Of *SAINT-WATCHING*,
Anne Morrow Lindbergh writes:

"I read it with delight, first for sheer readability and the pleasure one always has in this author's sharp and poetic feeling for words. Beyond this grace, Phyllis McGinley has managed here to combine scholarship, wit and wisdom in her humanly oriented accounts of the saints, both those inside and outside of the Christian calendar. Her book is immensely informative but never conventional. She not only 'chips away the plaster' in which, as she says, the saints too often are encased, but she allows us to see them as historically relevant to their times—and, many of them, astonishingly relevant to ours.

"In the end, she succeeds in convincing the reader that the essence of sanctity is never irrelevant to the times; all ages call forth their appropriate and desperately needed saintly figures. Here Florence Nightingale, Gandhi, and Pope John XXIII stand in the same company as Saint Francis and Saint Augustine."

Also by Phyllis McGinley

VERSE

On the Contrary
One More Manhattan
Pocketful of Wry
Husbands Are Difficult
Stones from a Glass House
A Short Walk from the Station
The Love Letters of Phyllis McGinley
Merry Christmas, Happy New Year
Times Three

PROSE

The Province of the Heart
Sixpence in Her Shoe
A Wreath of Christmas Legends

❀

Saint-Watching
by Phyllis McGinley

❀

IMAGE BOOKS
A DIVISION OF DOUBLEDAY & COMPANY, INC.
GARDEN CITY, NEW YORK

1974

Image Books edition by special arrangement with The Viking Press, Inc.

Image Books edition published September 1974

"Good Companions" originally appeared in *Mademoiselle*. "Saint-Watching" originally appeared as "A Little Grace" and "Holy Wit" as "The Wit of Saints" in *Vogue*. "The Quality of Mercy" originally appeared in *Woman's Day* magazine. Other selections have appeared in *The Critic, Horizon,* and *The Sign*.

Lines from "Running to Paradise" from *Collected Poems* by William Butler Yeats, Copyright 1916 by The Macmillan Company, renewed 1944 by Bertha Georgie Yeats, reprinted by permission of The Macmillan Company, New York, The Macmillan Company of Canada Ltd., and Mr. Michael B. Yeats.

Foreword

Books have wills of their own. This one bent me to its fancy and, over the years I worked on it, altered both my approach to the subject and my point of view. What began as simple good-humored entertainment turned into something a bit more serious than I had originally intended.

Not, I trust, that amusement is lacking in these pages. The Christian saints are a peculiar race and when one chips away the plaster in which they too often come encased one finds a set of people whose behavior can divert as well as edify. What I wished to do was to rescue them from their pious niches; to celebrate their eccentricities and persistent mortality.

At no time, of course, did I mean to ridicule them. They pleased me from the beginning, as they please me now, too much to denigrate. But I planned to take a more frivolous tone than I was able to maintain. The more I watched them the vaster seemed their accomplishments. Mere light-heartedness, the book decided for me, was not sufficient to contain their deeds and personalities. So, although I intended to describe them chiefly through quip and anecdote, I was forced to depict them in greater depth than was my first design.

To one attitude I did manage to hold fast. Any reader

expecting theological discussion will not find it here. Denominationalism, mysticism, religious tenets—all are still absent as I had determined. Nor is there anything but the barest mention of the God my protagonists all took for granted. I suppose that is rather like writing about Thomas Jefferson or Abraham Lincoln and leaving out politics. But my aim all along was to show the saints as earthly heroes rather than supernatural beings.

Only in the cases of Ignatius, Francis Borgia, and Paul have I attempted to do anything like a full-length portrait. But by permitting many of the same characters to turn up in various chapters under various guises of sanctity— that sanctity which is the world's strangest and highest form of genius—I trust that several others will be seen whole.

My hope is that even the nonbeliever will find them worth his while to stare at. They are, I repeat, a peculiar race, obscured for a very long while by curtains of legend and by pietistic, undiscriminating praise. Here, I trust, many of them will step down from their pedestals and let themselves be seen for the quirky and fiercely individualistic but humane and charming people they managed by their own efforts to become.

Contents

Foreword 9

RUNNING TO PARADISE

Saint-Watching 15
What Is a Saint? 25
In Defense of Saint Paul 39

ASPECTS OF SANCTITY

The Quality of Mercy 53
Ascent from Grandeur 62
Kind Men and Beasts 75
The Good Companions 86
A Cell of One's Own 98
Holy Wit 115

SAINTS BY NATIONALITY

Three against the Grain 127
The Wine of the Country 145
The Spaniard 166
The Saints of Ireland 191
Heroes without Halos 202

Afterword 223
Some Saints, Their Dates, and Feast Days 228
Index 231

Running to Paradise

The wind is old and still at play
While I must hurry upon my way
For I am running to Paradise.
        —William Butler Yeats

Saint-Watching

When I was seven years old I wanted to be a tight-rope dancer and broke my collar bone practicing on a child's-size high wire. At twelve I planned to become an international spy. At fifteen my ambition was the stage. Now in my sensible or declining years I would give anything (except my comforts, my customs, and my sins) to be a saint.

Of course there's a difference between this current daydream and my long-ago aspirations. I recognize it now for what it is, a mere sigh of the soul, the immemorial fantasy of middle age. I possess no more talent for conspicuous virtue than I ever had for aerial ballet. I have no head for heights. Still, the fancy not only pleases me but has given me an occupation. I know that I am a hero-worshiper; and saints have become the heroes I choose to stare at for the sheer excitement of their achievements as well as for their charms, crotchets, and eccentricities.

Because I was badly educated, I did not often encounter them as persons when I was younger. Oh, I had a vague knowledge that they existed. There was Francis, the Little Poor Man who called the swallows his sisters and who once tamed a wolf. I had heard about someone named Dominic who preached to the fish along the shore when no one came to hear his sermons in church. One

asked Jude for impossible wishes and Anthony for help
in locating missing fountain pens or charm bracelets. But
saints as real men and women I did not know at all.

It was only when I began reading history that I came
on the flesh and blood beings. At every turn and twist of
the years some saint emerged to enlarge or typify his age.
Saints, I found, had brought learning to barbarians and
guarded that light when it nearly flickered and went out
after Rome's fall. They had founded the first free hospitals,
invented progressive education, fought against slavery,
and (especially warming to me) given women a respectable place in society. I discovered Catherine of Siena, the
illiterate girl who lectured popes and nearly single-
handed brought a sort of peace to warring Italy. I came
across Lioba, who in the dark seventh century wrote
Latin verses and taught manners to rough German tribes.
There was Mother Marie (not yet beatified but made of
the stuff of saints) who ran her Indian missions in
Canada with the same sure hand she had once brought to
running her brother-in-law's carting business in France.
They all seemed men and women larger than life, and I
was forced to give them salutation. As my earlier heroes
fell away, when I left off giving my heart's entire devotion to acrobats or secret agents or fliers or the Cavalier
poets or the Florentine painters—when my sights, as it
were, sharpened—I took up saint-watching as other people
watch birds. For Tennyson was right. The old sentimental
line, "We needs must love the highest when we see it,"
is, like most sentimental sayings, perfectly true. Virtue is
man's Everest, and those who climb highest are most
worth admiring.

So, although I cannot imitate the saints, I can stare at
them, spying on them in their native coverts and attempting to follow their flights through my imperfect glass. I
classify them, I learn their names and their habits and the
color of their plumage. I track them down in books, doing
my best to flush them out from the forests of myth, the
secretive branches of history, taking care that I see them

as clearly as possible through the disconcerting thickets of hagiography where they too often take refuge.

I have to be careful there. Hagiography, the art of writing about the saints, is too often pious and sanctimonious rather than stirring. Biographers forget to do what Cromwell told his portraitist about painting warts and all. So those noble and natural creatures, born with the same faults and the same obstacles to virtue as the rest of us, are held up to display as both more and less than human. They seem never to have sinned, never to have faltered or stumbled. They were good when they were children. They were good in adolescence. They were good—one might even say goody-goody—through their mortal journeys. And where there is no struggle, there is no story and no edification for the likes of me. Yet as long as three centuries ago a great gentleman who earned his private halo, Francis de Sales, warned against reading sanctity into every act of the canonized. "There is no harm to the saints if their faults are shown as well as their virtues," he wrote to a friend. "But great harm is done to everybody by the hagiographers who slur over the faults, be it for the purposes of honoring the saints . . . or through fear of diminishing our reverence for their holiness."

With his silken common sense, Francis understood how much more profitable it was to revere a man grown good by his own efforts than one created sinless as the Angel Gabriel. Who could have known it better, since he, the most courteous, the most controlled, the most polished of Frenchmen struggled all his life (he tells us) against the quick, tigerish anger which was part of his heritage?

For the wonderful thing about saints is that they were *human.* They lost their tempers, got hungry, scolded God, were egotistical or testy or impatient in their turns, made mistakes and regretted them. Still they went on doggedly blundering toward heaven. And they won sanctity partly by willing to be saints, not because they encountered no temptation to be less.

Occasionally there was one for whom the struggle

seems to have been easy, like Thomas Aquinas, fat and
kind and heavy with thought. It is impossible to discover
genuine meanness or sin even in the boy at school whom
they called "the dumb ox." But Francis of Assisi was a
gay rake and prodigal before he gave all he had to the
poor and took up his staff and sandals. The Portuguese
John of God was a gambler, a drunkard, and a mercenary
soldier until he was forty. Then all those talents one would
have thought spent and wasted he gathered up into his
hands and showered on the sick poor. Mary of Egypt was
a harlot like Magdalene before her. And the most tempestuous of them all was Saint Augustine, whose famous
cry of the heart, "God make me chaste, but not yet," rings
down through the years with the authentic human note.
There have been, among the saints, thieves, beggars, and
vagabonds, even men who killed. That they turned the
fury of their impulses toward good and toward God instead of toward the evil they knew perfectly well existed,
is their accolade. It is the reason that spying on them is
such a satisfying pursuit. Not much of the glory rubs off
on the pursuer but then a bird-watcher does not expect
to learn how to fly. His, like mine, is a spectator's delight.
The glory of the watched is nearly enough to satisfy him.
Moreover, he is always coming across unsuspected domestic glimpses of the quarry, glimpses which put him on
easy terms with it.

For instance, I take my chief pleasure in the touching
or the extravagant I keep discovering in the biographies.
I love Francis Xavier because of many things—his zeal,
his charity, his footsore journeys across the world to bring
light to the pagan. But I cherish him chiefly because his
nature was so affectionate that, thousands of miles away
from home and his brother Jesuits, he cut the signatures
from their letters to him and pinned them inside his habit
next to his heart.

The great Thomas of Aquino, whom I have already
mentioned, held the whole philosophical world on his
massive shoulders. I, too, can admire the architecture of

his intellect and repeat with amused awe the best-known story about him: that in the middle of a state dinner given by King Louis IX he remained so absorbed in speculation that he brought his enormous fist down suddenly on the table as he blurted out, "And that settles the Manichees!" But another comment of his is less famous and more warming. Because he was shy and quiet and forever thinking, one does not usually consider him a sociable man. Yet, "No possession is joyous without a companion," he said, and remarked wistfully about gardens that "Notwithstanding the beasts and the plants, one can be lonely there."

Teresa of Avila is so famous and so often quoted that nearly everyone can cite one of her tart sayings. (She was also so holy that in her ecstasies of prayer, it is said, she was forced sometimes to hold on to the altar rail to keep herself from floating embarrassingly upward.) But she appeals to me in her busy humanity, in her traipsing about Spain from foundation to foundation, loving God, children, and her friends with the same zest. "I have no defense against affection," she said. "I could be bribed with a sardine." There was nothing smug about Teresa. I treasure her rejoinder to a visitor who found her happily eating a partridge someone had sent her. The visitor was scandalized. A holy woman actually enjoying her food! What would people think? "Let them think what they please," said Teresa. "There is a time for partridge and a time for penance."

And that settled that particular Manichee.

Perhaps I love my heroes for the wrong reasons. (But then I am only a watcher.) Take Saint Boniface for one. The most famous of the early English monks, he did great works of proselyting the heathen and of establishing the Christian faith in Europe. But I remember him for the strength of his friendships. Although he never drank anything stronger than water himself, one finds him writing to Egbert, Archbishop of York, "Instead of the kiss which I am prevented from giving you, I am sending by the bearer of this letter, two little kegs of wine. As you love me, I beg you to use it for a day of rejoicing with your friends."

A willingness to let others be comfortable while living austerely oneself seems to me the height of generosity. Boniface reminds me a bit of dear old William Law. Law was not a saint, not even a member of the church which grants official nimbi. He is remembered now chiefly because he wrote a book called *A Serious Call to a Devout and Holy Life,* which strongly influenced John Wesley. He was an English clergyman, chaplain to the Gibbon family and tutor to the historian. I love him for his kindness to that rather formidable family. Law was a practical mystic who rose every day at five in the morning, said his prayers, did his meditations, milked four cows which he had bought and installed in the barns there, and with the milk made gruel for the beggars and the poor who crowded to his gate. Then and only then, at about nine a.m., when his own tasks were finished, did he wake the rest of the household for their prayers and their breakfast. What early-riser among us can so gently endure the slugabed? (He also, I recall, went about the countryside buying up larks and linnets in cages and releasing them to the province of the air.)

I enjoy Philip Neri for his jokes and his riddles as well as for his piety. I like Hilda of Whitby because in an age little given to personal daintiness she bathed every day. I salute Thomas More, who taught his daughters Greek and Latin in the time when girls were considered unworthy of being educated. I even like Saint Jerome because he was so cross that other desert monks found it difficult to get on with him—surely a severe penance for a man running to paradise. And who could resist Blessed Fra Angelico, of whom Michelangelo exclaimed, "He must have gone to Paradise for his models"? That little monk painted only as God directed him and never touched a picture after it was finished because that would not have been His will. I smile at Vasari's remark about him: "He was never seen in anger by the friars, which is a great thing, and seems to be almost impossible to believe." But Vasari, inspired gossip that he was, went on believing it because it seems to have been true. And indeed, it *is* a great thing to be both a saint and an artist. The one career would seem to dissolve the other, each being in its way an exclusive dedication.

Writing, on the other hand, seems less difficult to reconcile with virtue although, like Vasari, I find it "almost impossible to believe." Many of the saints wrote like angels, from Augustine himself to Francis de Sales, patron now of journalists (and what a comedown the journalism of today must be to him, most exquisite of stylists!). Teresa, John of the Cross, Ambrose, surly Jerome, Anthony, Dominic, old Boniface, Bede the historian, Columba the poet, Thomas More, and a hundred others were distinguished writers, sometimes true geniuses. One of my pets among the authors is Elisha, an early Desert Father, who caroled like a thrush and is credited with writing thirty thousand songs. If Elisha's claim seems excessive, I am not abashed. There is much in hagiography that sounds absurd, and I relish the absurd along with the magnificent.

Some of the absurd is being lost to us. The Vatican, after all these centuries, has finally cast a cold eye on some two hundred saints early listed in the Calendar. Finding that some of them may never have existed and that the rest have become too encrusted with unattested miracles to be believable, it has either dropped them entirely or deprived them of their mandatory feast days. Most of them were so obscure as to cause no furor. But three famous wonder workers have lost their right to "universal veneration," and we shall miss them. They are Valentine, Nicholas, and Christopher, patron of travelers of every faith.

No matter. The world will keep Valentine's Day just as it has done for so long. Since Nicholas has chiefly meant Santa Claus to most of us, he, too, will be yearly remem-

bered. As for Christopher, I suspect his imagined image
will still decorate thousands of medals in thousands of
careering motor cars. Folk tales die hard; they also carry
their own antic significances. I, for one, intend to go on
reading the old Calendar, being amused by legend nearly
as much as I am in love with fact.

I like to be told that a legendary Saint Gothard is supposed to have hung his cloak on a sunbeam when he could
not find a hook, and that a genuine Nicholas the Pilgrim
was a shepherd who kept his sheep calm by singing them
the *"Kyrie Eleison."* I am fond of Sabrinus, who understood
the language of birds, and preached to them note by note;
and of Datius, who made fun of the Devil and vanquished
him by mockery. It takes a saint to turn the devil's weapon
against him so skillfully. The first biographers wrote in the
earliest days of faith, when miracles seemed to be all
around them, happening every day. So if they pinned an
extra ornament or two on their subjects, it was only in a
spirit of good will, a sort of spiritual metaphor. Besides,
who could invent a character such as Christina the Astonishing? This saint was particularly charitable and served
the poor and the ill with devotion, but she had a failing
—she could not bear the stench of unwashed human flesh.
Since her parishioners consisted chiefly of medieval peasants, their aura was constantly with her, and it seems a
peculiar asceticism indeed that kept her persevering in
their care. There she would be, binding up the wounds
of some villager or tending a sick farm wife when suddenly her delicate nose would become so helplessly of-
fended that she must rush out of doors to draw a breath
of clean air. She was constantly begging her less fastidious
friends not to press too near. Still, she went on dispensing
charity until she died. It was only at her own funeral that
she misbehaved. So many people crowded into the church
to pay their respects that the coffin with poor Christina in
it went bounding up to the top of the building in one last
desperate attempt to escape the odor of humanity. It
seems that the priest had to turn from the altar and order

her to descend from the rafters, "which she did meekly."
One hopes she now walks among lilies.

But if I take pleasure in the eccentric and absurd, I am
not an entirely impartial watcher. Some of the most
mighty and influential saints rather put me off. I acknowl-
edge their virtue. But I cannot love Saint Paula, for one,
with my whole heart, because, strong-minded Roman
matron that she was, she left her children behind her when
she followed Jerome to celibacy in the desert. I suppose
the boy and the girl, Toxotius and Rufiana, had relatives
and tutors to look after them, for Paula was very wealthy
indeed. And I suppose, too, there is not much difference
between deserting your children and eloping from your
parents' roof like Clare, when she took the Franciscan
habit one starry night in Assisi. I simply do not find in
Paula the tenderness one expects from saints.

Charles Borromeo is too steely for my taste, Rose of
Lima too extravagant in her mortifications, and Theresa of
Lisieux too incorrigibly girlish to give me comfort. But the
rewarding thing about watching saints is that there are so
many of them, far more than enough to go around. And
for every fanatic or bore among them there are a thousand
delightful ones to adopt as friends.

There is Irish Bridget, who gave away everything in her
own house and in the house of her father and eventually
of the king himself, and to any beggar passing by. She
even managed to make the forces of nature cooperate with
her in giving. For the story goes that once when she and
her community had spent a hard long day feeding the
poor—when they had disposed of every loaf of bread,
every egg from their hens, every pear from their trees—
word came that the Seven Bishops of Cabinteely were
on their way to visit her and would expect hospitality. The
nuns were atwitter. What would their reverences think of
a convent so stripped of food for the episcopal table?
Bridget didn't turn a hair. "Go out and ask the hens kindly
to lay more eggs," she told one sister. "Speak to the trees
—see what they have left in the way of fruit," she advised

another. "Talk gently to the cows and beg them for a little milk."

She herself went into the kitchen, poked the fire, and opened the oven, and there on the hearth sat a number of beautifully baked loaves, hot and crusty. The hens cackled and gave eggs. The cows let down more milk. The trees shook their branches and apples and pears fell into the nuns' aprons. And the seven bishops that evening vowed they had never in their lives sat down to a handsomer feast.

There is, on the more historic side, Philip Neri, expounding one of the basic tenets of progressive education: "If you wish to be obeyed, you must appear not to be giving orders."

There is Pius X, who was a worry to his valet because he *would* give away all his shirts. There is Thomas the Doubter, who ennobled his fault of skepticism by admitting it and repenting, and who seems very close to us in this era. There are the glorious strugglers like Joan of Arc, and the great preachers, like Robert Bellarmine, who loved the "undeserving poor." There are the martyrs and the simple men of prayer, the ignorant and the learned, the stern and the mild. There are, to return to my first figure of speech, all the birds of field and air to be watched —thrushes, robins, wrens, doves, hummingbirds, woodpeckers, even cheeky sparrows like Don John Bosco, who set up his homes for boys by sheer exuberance and effrontery.

And if I cannot learn how to fly like them or sing like them, I can learn a little of their ways. I can study the courtesy of Francis, the generosity of Bridget, the unpretentiousness of Philip, the self-command of Augustine, the kindness of Thomas, or that merriment in the face of adversity which was peculiarly Teresa's. It gives me, I repeat, an occupation, and I hope it will at length give me a little grace.

What Is a Saint?

I cannot repeat often enough that saints are not angels. They enter the world as human beings; arrive as ennobled or disfigured by mortality as the rest of us.

It is because they must wear to the end of their lives the same imperfect human garment which clothes mankind that they catch at our minds. Therefore I am not alone in my occupation of saint-watching. Ours is an age of violence and disbelief. But in spite of that, or perhaps because of it, the earth's interest in virtuous accomplishment is stronger now than it has been at any time since the Age of Reason began ousting religion from its seat of authority. God may be dead insofar as theological concepts no longer direct political and economic affairs. But His heroes still interest the race. They are quoted by columnists, cited by historians, their names taken not always in vain by novelists, biographers, and agnostic tractarians. Thomas More was not long ago the protagonist of a noble play, a notable film; as was Becket twice in a decade. Joan of Arc never fails the playwright. Not long ago in the sober *New York Times* an editorial recommended that in our dealings with nature we try, for the sake of conservation, to become more like Francis of Assisi who considered all living creatures his brothers.

In times of crisis we need saints; and we often breed

them, too. They appeared by hundreds in the first centuries of Christianity when Europe was struggling out of nearly universal darkness into what then passed for the light of civilization. They flourished during the Reformation on both sides of the conflict. Wherever and whenever an evil has existed, from slave-trading to the miseries of famine and war, saints have sprung up to mitigate those evils. They may well be rising among us now, preparing to lead us out of the onrushing night which so threateningly descends. As a matter of fact, I think I number two or three among my acquaintances.

But just how does one recognize them? What exactly is a saint? I take on the task of answering my own questions with more recklessness than scholarship. And however I define them will be open to argument, will be no more than a theory achieved by personal scrutiny. After all, even the Catholic Church, which almost alone among religions hands out halos for "heroic virtue" much as nations grant medals for conspicuous gallantry in battle, finds them difficult to pinpoint. For nearly a thousand years it has owned an apparatus for canonization complete with petitions from the dead candidate's sponsors and well-wishers, a dossier of his good deeds, and a Devil's Advocate whose function it is to pick flaws in the case at issue. (This apparatus for the first time in centuries is currently in the process of revision.) Yet while they lived the very saints which the Church eventually honors may have been suspect to the same establishment. Ignatius Loyola, founder of the Jesuits, was eight times imprisoned by the Inquisition. Teresa of Avila ran afoul of it, as did Francis Borgia, John of the Cross, and a multitude of others. It was fifty years after his death before the writings of Thomas Aquinas, now the basis for much churchly doctrine, were declared safe for the orthodox. The best of saints walked a constant tightrope, teetering (as did Pascal, who still remains unhaloed) just above the abyss of heresy.

At once so alike and so diverse are the personalities of

my heroes that no pope or bishop or even fellow saint can say dogmatically, "Do this, renounce that, and you will be called blessed." Some have tried. Scholastica, great Benedict's sister, announced back in the sixth century that one had only to "will to be a saint." Theresa of Lisieux explained that she herself would make the attempt "in a little way" and that she would probably succeed because "the good God would not inspire unattainable desires." Evidently optimism is a holy attribute. But on the whole we see results, not methods.

We have a record of one attempt to discover the operations of sanctity which is as diverting to us as it was frustrating to the watcher. The subject under investigation was Francis de Sales, and his arrogantly curious observer was Jean Pierre Camus, Bishop of Belley. There seems to have been no planned mischief in the trick the Bishop used, but there was certainly bad taste. For what he did was drill a hole in the wall of his bedroom in the episcopal residence so that he could spy on his host when Francis thought himself alone. Camus was not an enemy to Francis. He loved and revered the charming Savoyard who was working such miracles of apostleship in his hard-bitten Genevan diocese; who was becoming a legend in France for holiness, charity, and—of even greater importance to the French—an elegant prose style. The Bishop of Belley leaned on the Bishop of Geneva for advice, friendship, and entertainment. But he meant to be de Sales' biographer. He was ridden by his Boswellian need to find out more about this saint-in-training than the public image showed. One trusts, too, that he hoped to learn a little about the road a good man might travel toward perfection.

And what did Camus discover? Only that Francis was the same privately as he was in company. That he crept out of bed early and quietly in the mornings so as not to wake his servant. That he prayed, wrote, answered his letters, read his office, slept, and prayed again. The beautiful manners, the unruffled compassion, the courtesy and humility were on display at the peephole as they had been in the pulpit or at the dinner table. There was no secret man. Poor Camus, for all his hours of staring, learned nothing about sanctity except its outward face, which he knew already. He went on to write his book, anyway, as biographers do, becoming an author rather than a holy person.

If the Bishop of Belley could not anatomize sainthood, having been its companion, it must be next to indefinable. That strange valor is as baffling as any other form of genius.

Indeed, what are saints *except* geniuses—geniuses who bring to their works of virtue all the splendor, eccentricity, effort, and dedication that lesser talents bring to music or poetry or painting? William James in *Varieties of Religious Experience* uses the same word when he wishes to pin down his mystics. But he used it in a narrower sense than do I. His epithet had nineteenth-century scientific overtones. A "genius" to James meant less an exaltation of some human gift than an aberration, a departure from the norm. My term implies extraordinary ability. Saints seem to me men or women with an added dimension. Like musicians, painters, poets, they are human beings but obsessed ones. They are obsessed by goodness and by God as Michelangelo was obsessed by line and form, as Shakespeare was bewitched by language, Beethoven by sound. And like other geniuses they used mortal means to contrive their masterpieces.

A certain striving after virtue is native to man. Most of us inherit (or acquire) a moral sense as we inherit other capacities which the genius simply owns in enlarged form. Without being Mozarts we may still have an ear for music and be able to carry a tune. Without rivaling Keats, we may yet depend on language as a tool or write a cadenced sentence. So, without any expectation of emulating the Little Poor Man, the majority of us are quite willing to empty our pockets for blind beggars, support a just cause, be merciful to animals, and love, as nearly as possible, our

exasperating neighbor. Only monsters rejoice in wickedness. When the race throws up such a monster, he can
bring down half a world. In this century there have been
spectacular examples of viciousness and we have seen
them plain. But the mass of men, to paraphrase Thoreau,
live lives of quiet heroism. If only to attract affection, we
would like to be good, or at least to seem admirable in
the fashion of the time. Flawed as man is, in general he
plods doggedly on down some path he dimly perceives to
be a righteous one. The trouble with most of us is that
our souls are not strong enough to withstand the corroding
effect of daily living. Fatigue and despair nibble away our
good intentions. Lack of a night's sleep can destroy a
resolution against peevishness; business troubles consume
kindness. Saints master their environment as we do not.

Still, for all our talk about the sinfulness of the world
and despite publicized examples of cupidity or wantonness or self-indulgence, the average citizen of earth is so
frequently rich in patience, generosity, and gallantry that
it breaks the heart. Evil exists but virtue (even if diluted)
is more abundant.

The saints differ from us in their exuberance, the excess
of our human talents. Moderation is not their secret. It is
in the wildness of their dreams, the desperate vitality of
their ambitions, that they stand apart from ordinary men
of good will.

At least it would seem so at first glance. But if they
merely possess exaggerations of our best qualities, is there
no absolute link among them? How do we tag with the
same label men and women so various as Rose of Lima,
with her tears and preposterous mortifications, and Avilan
Teresa, who taught her nuns to dance for joy in the cloister?
There have been war-mongering saints like Bernard and
saints who preached only pacifism like Martin of Tours,
the first known conscientious objector. Although Martin
had been an officer in the Roman Legions, he refused to
fight after his conversion and was imprisoned by the

Emperor Julian. I wonder that the young men who burn their draft cards do not invoke him now.

There was Jerome (and because he was such a difficult saint he *will* keep cropping up in this book), who could scarcely stir without the feminine advice of Saint Paula; and there was Dalmatius Moner, who "with women would not talk at all except over his shoulder." A number were hermits like Anthony of Egypt, eyeing the social scene of his day with disfavor. And then there were gregarious saints who lived serenely in the world, like Francis de Sales himself, like Alphonsus de Liguori. The latter, for instance, was very fond of music, and since the only place he could hear it easily was on the stage of his native Naples, which often featured licentious tableaux, he found a way around his predicament—rather a wily one, too. He had the dubious advantage of being near-sighted. So when he went to the theater, he sat well back in a box away from the stage and, once the curtain went up, promptly took off his spectacles. He could listen without seeing and thus "come to no harm." I think he deserves sanctification for the innocent way he enjoyed himself without thundering against the stage and so destroying Neapolitan pleasure. Not all good men are so tolerant.

There have been esthetic lovers of this sweet earth like Grimonia, of whom it was said that "the contemplation of the beauty of created things often brought her to the state of ecstasy." Opposed to her is dear, zealous Francis Xavier, that indefatigable missionary, who traveled through a dozen kingdoms with no more eye for the scenery than a migrating bird.

"Beauty," writes James Brodrick in his biography of Francis, "whether created by God or fashioned by the genius of man, seems never to have touched his preoccupied soul. . . . It was a defect in his nature. . . . Of poetry's silver and gold Francis might own hardly a sixpence, but he had other riches to spend on men with an almost divine extravagance, and there grew in him a beauty of holiness, often a terrible beauty. Where art stops short, unable to say anything more, then the grandeur of the saint begins." Brodrick's paragraph helps fit together the pieces of the jigsaw puzzle which is the picture of the saint-as-genius.

For one has constantly to be reminded that sanctity does not always entail esthetic or even intellectual gifts. Celestial talent does for the most part accompany intellect. There are whole armies of learned saints, like Augustine and Albert the Great and Aquinas, like Bede the historian who is the only Englishman mentioned by Dante in the *"Paradiso."* Thomas More and de Sales make good reading still. There have been composers and artists, writers and philosophers aplenty. They are so numerous that we take them for granted like Fra Angelico, or ignore them as we do Tutilo, who, hidden away in the monastery of Saint Gall, was "poet, orator, architect, painter, sculptor, metal worker, but most of all a superb musician."

Then, as if to display the broad spectrum of sanctity, there are ignorant or clumsy-minded saints like prattling Theresa of Lisieux or the Curé d'Ars. One cannot imagine choosing either to enliven a salon. There is, for good measure, Blessed Bertilla Boscardin, elevated to beatitude only in 1922. She was called "the Goose" in her Italian village of Brendola, and had a hard time persuading the authorities she possessed enough sense to enter a convent. "I am a goose," she told her superiors, "but teach me to be a saint." And among the pots and pans and potato peelings she arrived at her goal.

We do not have to walk socially with saints to feel their impact. The beatific vision has to be high but not necessarily broad. Their sights are centered on a peak so Alpine that only an eagle, a telescope, or one of their own kind can make out the landmarks they stare at. It is why few of them would make altogether agreeable company. Many are loveable, but not all; and none, I expect, was cozy. We feel most at ease with faulty people like ourselves. A leaning toward gossip, a touch of sloth or egotism—those are endearing qualities in our friends which make us seem at

home with them. Brodrick rightly calls Francis Xavier
"preoccupied." So are all the holy regiments.

I think now of Dr. Johnson's comment on John Wesley.
"Wesley's conversation is good," said the august Doctor.
"But he is never at leisure. He is always obliged to go at
a certain hour. This is disagreeable to a man who loved
to fold his legs and have out his talk as I do." Wesley mel-
lowed as he aged, but he was always a man in a rush
toward heaven. So are most saints, which is why they are
inspirational rather than comradely.

Still, even the sociability is available. For sanctity has a
variety as infinite as Cleopatra's. But, variety or no, one
pattern comes clear. And here I begin at last my own
definition. They have a common quality which sets them
off from the rest of us as Bach is set off from a composer
of television jingles. Yes, they are all geniuses. Yes, again,
they are all excessive. But they are something else. They
are literal. Literalness is the fork in the upward road where
they part company with ordinary people.

And it is the Gospels, the solid, explicit Word which
they take literally.

What does that Word tell us? Nurse the sick, clothe
the naked, feed the hungry, comfort the afflicted. Sell all
you have and give to the poor. Go forth and preach to all
nations. Turn the other cheek. Return good for evil. Love
God and your neighbor as yourself. Those are soul-stirring
slogans which most of us absent-mindedly attend to and
admire as we admire all lofty phrases. We even try to
follow them in moderation. We agree that charity covers
a multitude of sins and besides is deductible on the Income Tax. We comfort the afflicted in committee or sub-
scribe to a fund for the relief of earthquake victims a
hemisphere away. We take flowers to hospitals, speak with
friendship to the folk next door, and give away our old
clothes to the deprived.

But the saints, I repeat, are not moderate.

"Sell all you have and give to the poor" to them is a
commandment which means exactly what it says. Over

and over they strip themselves of every worldly possession, as Francis did, as he trained his disciples to do. When Giles, one of his first associates, was walking with him on a country road, the two were accosted by a beggar woman. Francis owned only his habit, which he had made out of a peasant's discarded gown and a bit of rope for a belt. But Giles wore a coat.

"Give it to her," said Francis as naturally as he might have commented, "It's a fine morning."

And Giles was launched on the Franciscan way.

Francis is only the most famous of hundreds. I expect to talk about him again and again, for he is almost a symbol of holiness. He was also a poet, his life an irresistible canticle of holy joy, and the world knows him better than any other virtue-lover except Gandhi. But when he gave away his food, his clothes, his books, and his heart to any man he encountered on the road, he was following a trail as old as Christendom.

Just as regularly as folk tales begin "Once upon a time," so half the biographies of saints start with "He first sold his estates and goods for the benefit of the poor."

The gentle Desert Fathers: Martin, who shared his cloak with a stranger; William Pinchon, who called the poor his "treasures"; Cyran the Abbot, who distributed alms with such recklessness when he inherited his father's estate that he was for a while in danger of being "restrained as a lunatic"; Vincent Palloti, who many times came home half naked because he had parted with his clothes—the list reads like a wild litany. Francis is only the best known of the give-aways.

Laurence O'Toole, the last saint of Ireland, who was prince, diplomat, Lord Bishop, laughed aloud on his deathbed when a friend suggested that he make a will. "A queer thing, me with a will," said Laurence. "For I have not a penny in the world to leave to anybody."

Charity is the saints' signature and later in this book I shall devote a chapter wholly to that facet of their characters. For it is one talent they uniformly share. Nor do they mind whether or not their good works are appreciated. We non-geniuses like to receive thanks for our efforts. Saints squander their love on the undeserving and the ungrateful. They ask nothing, not even appreciation, in return.

So it goes with the rest of the Gospel code.

Preach to all nations? Of course. So exhilarated by glad tidings are they that they must run, run, carrying their own hope to the most remote corners of the earth. Thomas and Peter began the trek. Paul, as we shall see, continued it, restless and vocal, a scrawny, lean, indomitable little traveler "in journeyings often, in peril of waters . . . in hunger and thirst." And from him stems an army of imitators.

We have our Xavier, undaunted in the Orient, ringing his little bell to call small heathens to prayers. We have a Jogues enduring his martyrdom among the most savage of American Indians. Or we have a Peter Claver, combining evangelism with charity while he preached in the West Indies to the Negro slaves and their less willing-to-listen masters. "For," says Butler's *Lives of the Saints* with perhaps unconscious irony, "he did not regard even the most brutal of the slave-owners as despicable barbarians beyond the mercy of God. They also had souls to be saved, no less than the Negroes." From Peter through Boniface to the Maryknoll Missioners of this decade, evangelism runs like a gold thread through all the annals.

In the same spirit of literal undertaking, saints spend their lives and their burning abilities on every sort of necessity they find at hand. They care for lepers, foundlings, prisoners of war, idiots, orphans. They defend Jews as did Hugh of Lincoln, who, singlehanded, cowed armed and angry mobs in England of the twelfth century or sheltered fugitives in his episcopal palace. They found hospitals. They teach the ignorant. Like Raymund Nonnatus they give themselves up as hostages for the ransom of slaves and captives. Imagine the most enormous of the corporal acts of mercy, and some saint or whole contingent of saints has committed it.

Do good to those that hate you? There is the example of Joan of Orvieto, of whom it was said, "Anyone who wants Sister Joan's prayers should do her a bad turn." We have an Ignatius walking a hundred miles out of his way in winter to nurse a man he heard had fallen sick—the same man who a few weeks before had stolen Ignatius's small store of money. Or we have a Saint Spiridion, who, having interrupted a gang of thieves attempting one night to carry off his sheep, set them free and gave them a ram "lest they should have been up all night for nothing."

Or else the benign people take literally the commandment to "pray without ceasing" and turn hermit or, like Benedict, found monasteries where contemplation is lifted into an art and purpose of life. My pet among the prayerful is Blessed Mariolino, who spent so much time in soliciting God's mercy for sinners that after his death heavy calluses were found on both knees.

More than anything else saints take without one grain of salt the most difficult of commandments—that one must "die to self."

Much has been made of this last feat, for from it stem their strange austerities so often repellent to this self-indulgent generation. The penances of such a figure as Margaret of Cortona, who after having "lived nine years with a lover" asserted that "between this body and me must be a struggle till death," seem to us ridiculous. But those old saints used penances not as an end but as a means. Brother Ass, the body, had to be tamed, had to be bridled and saddled before he could be ridden on God's work. And to simple, literal-minded holy people of early times, the means were often fasts or thirsts or hairshirts or years spent in the wilderness. They were like athletes at training tables, strengthening not their muscles but their souls. For what we must remember above all is that they are flesh and blood, as liable to temptation as we—perhaps, because of their intensity of feeling, even more.

"Sit on the other side of the table, please, Madam," one of the Fathers told a pretty penitent. "I am not yet an old man."

Pious biographers used to forget this essential truth and tended to paint out all the flaws in their subjects. They liked their saints made entirely of plaster, like the remarkable child of legend who at three days old addressed an eloquent sermon to his parents and then took off for Paradise. The facts are quite otherwise. They might not be converted from outright brigandage as was Moses the Black, or from piracy like English Gudric. But they began life with man's ordinary complement of faults. Raymond Lull, that charming apostle to the Moors, decorous and mild as he became, was in his youth, according to his own admission, "shameless in pursuit of any new face that attracted me." Even the great Monsieur Vincent de Paul, the selfless man whose very name has become a synonym for charity, described himself to a friend as "by nature of a bilious temperament and very subject to anger." All through their lives they continued to be human, to stumble, repent, and sometimes even stumble again. The picking themselves up is the triumph. Out of their frailties they made virtues, like Mechtildis, who "fought her hasty tongue until she became a model of tact," or Augustine himself, who never quenched his fire but only made it burn brightly for humanity.

And even the harshest of their penances were undertaken not out of hatred but for love.

We talk a good deal about the need for love these days. The word is bandied about by psychiatrists, pediatricians, and the more emotional novelists. But it is the great secret which saints have known all along. They are possessed by it. Even the weakest of them, the most fallible—a Jerome, for instance, of whom someone remarked while he observed a picture of the crotchety old man in the act of striking his breast with a stone, "You do well to carry that stone, for without it you would never have been canonized"—even he knew the burden of an affection too great to be contained.

Gentle Hugh the Great, who ruled the Abbey of Cluny with so tender a hand, was said to have "loved in their due order, God above all, his neighbor equally with himself, and the world beneath his feet." It seems the aptest description of a saint that man can invent.

A friend of mine, a believer but not an extraordinarily religious woman, told me once that she had, while attending church, a most extraordinary experience. Suddenly and for no apparent reason she was swept by a wave of love. "I'm a self-contained sort," she said, "and not much given to emotion. But this was something outside myself. For a brief time I knew what it was to cherish the world. Everything seemed endearing. I loved the pastor, the congregation, the wriggling children back of me, the woman kneeling beside me, the man in the seat ahead coughing into his handkerchief. I wanted to hug them all. The feeling left me almost as soon as it had come, but it is something I wish never to forget."

Her revelation lasted only a moment. It is probably at such a pitch that saints spend their lives. Love makes them unique. For it they forsake the world or rove about in it, give up their possessions, wear themselves out with generosity and subdue their bodies to its service. It accounts for their eccentric gestures—Francis embracing a leper, Peter kissing the sores of the sick. It accounts for their enormous compassion, for what Bernanos calls their "strong, gentle pity." God-struck, love-struck, they accomplish miracles of charity beside which all other works of art seem unimportant.

But what about real miracles? people ask. What about healing the sick with a touch, finding lost objects, turning bread into roses? Such stories are festoons hung by the credulous about saints' necks after death, when they can no longer defend themselves. While they lived, most of them disappointingly refused to perform marvels. The only miracles they made were their own lives.

I have said I number two or three incipient saints among my acquaintances. One of them spends himself among impoverished Negroes of the South, one wears himself out in Northern slums, the third (completely without personal possessions) by some sleight of hand and heart feeds and lodges hundreds of Bowery derelicts each week.

For since every generation has its peculiar evils, it is modern injustices that modern saints will work to overcome. They will not necessarily nurse lepers or ransom prisoners of war. It is prejudice, drug addiction, neediness, and ignorance against which they will launch their fiery energies. They may suffer persecution and hardship like their predecessors—may spend patient hours in picket lines or patient months in jail. Not the poor of the roadside but the poor of underprivileged communities will engross them, and whenever a down-and-outer gets into a breadline they will be ladling out the food. They will bind up wounds on battlefields, teach the illiterate to read, comfort the old and the unhappy.

They may be believers or agnostics. But they will all be men and women who take the Gospels literally.

In Defense of Saint Paul

All heroes have their alternate periods of adulation and eclipse. Saints and other geniuses are no different from the rest. If such a figure as a Greco or a Shakespeare can suffer decline in popularity from century to century, it is not strange that the sage or holy man most honored in one generation is suspect in another.

The theology of Augustine, once the very pillar of Catholic authority, is today tarred with the brush of predestination. Thomas Aquinas seems fading a little, not in the force of his personality (for that dear man can beguile the most determined atheist with the enchantment of his life) but in the force of his Arguments. There was a time when Calvin towered over the world as the overwhelming figure of the Protestant movement. Now one can scarcely persuade a scholar to say a good word for him even though he lived, according to his lights, a life of complete piety. Of course he *did* burn Servetus, and for that he is remembered when his virtues are forgotten. (While I was doing a bit of research on the Genevan lawmaker, I couldn't find even in theological libraries a genuine piece of praise for him; and it amused me that I discovered the most complete and respectful article on his work in, of all books, the *Catholic Encyclopedia*.)

In an even more important way, Saint Paul, the greatest

Christian influence who ever existed, apart from Christ Himself, currently has his detractors. He is criticized for having modeled the early Church in his own image; for having imprinted on it too strict a taint of Puritanism; for following too authoritarian a method of handling his congregations. Even his anguished boast that he has been "all things to all men" is called hypocritical. Chiefly, however, he is castigated for being the original antifeminist and for having left *that* crippling legacy to Christianity for all time. "Let your women keep silent in the churches" has become a sort of rallying cry against him. So has the letter in which he admonishes the Corinthians (his enemies say the admonishment is grudging) that "it is better to marry than burn."

In short, Paul is out of style. Some gentler apostle, less hortatory, seems to suit these times in which freedom of behavior is the only virtue many a reformer acknowledges.

Yet to reread his Epistles is to fall in love all over again with this burning architect of our Christian heritage. And to study with some scrupulousness the society of the first century, particularly the Judaic portion of it, is to realize how temperate was his advice if not his nature and how nearly supernatural the work he accomplished.

For the wonderful thing about Paul is that we really know him. Not necessarily the total Paul and all the turns and twists of his spirit. After all, we have only his replies, not the correspondence which induced them; and a one-sided correspondence is always subject to misinterpretation. There were so many questions, so many answers, so many gaps that must be filled in by the imagination. As Ronald Knox has pointed out in his fascinating history of heresies, *Enthusiasm,* "The mind of Paul has been misunderstood all down the centuries; there is no aberration of Christianity which does not point to him as the source of its inspiration." But if his doctrine has apparent inconsistencies, the figure of the human Paul seems as real as the man next door.

The other Apostles are vague by comparison. The Acts

of the Apostles gives us their occupations and a bit of primitive biography. We know that Luke was a physician and a Gentile, that Peter denied the Lord and was forgiven, and that Thomas doubted and was healed of his doubt. But Paul in his letters (written several years before the Gospels) is a living, breathing person. He exhorts, he complains, begs for assurances from his congregations that they hold him in affection, sends his thanks to "Priscilla and Aquila," recounts his travels and his hardships, scolds his parishes roughly in one paragraph and consoles them in the next; even while he answers the queries and settles the disputes of his fledgling communities. For those who think of Paul as no more than a puritanical if eloquent preacher must remember that some of his severest advice (as well as some of his tenderest) was set down in response to reports of schisms and quarrels arising among the very new members of this very new sect. And they must recall also that these replies had to be tailored to the national and religious origins of the devotees. It was, after all, a form of Judaism which he was teaching—Judaism with a Promise fulfilled—and it had to be taught to people as unlike as the Jews of Jerusalem, the turbulent Romans of Rome itself, and the lax pagans of Corinth and Thessaly. All had to be somehow united in morality, peace, order.

The familiar story never loses its excitement. Paul was a Roman citizen, brought up in Hellenic Tarsus, speaking Greek and surrounded by Greek culture. But, most important, he was Saul, the orthodox Pharisee, a tentmaker and a rabbi, so fierce against Jewish heresy that his persecution of the Christians once meant terror to the countryside. It was at Saul's feet that the witnesses "laid their clothes" while they stoned the first martyr, Stephen. His crusading zeal sent him to Damascus to ferret out in the synagogues there any practicing Christians so that "whether they were men or women, he might bring them bound into Jerusalem." Then, of course, came the light on the road and the three-day blindness, and Saul the hunter becomes Paul the Apostle, hunted in turn the rest of his extraordinary life.

He is, as I have said, the prototype for all later saints. Everything is consistent. First the conversion, then the human hesitations and timidities to be overcome, next the missionary work and the deeds of mercy, and finally and always the struggle for total submerging of self in the Other.

On the other hand, to speak of "conversion" is almost a misnomer. Paul never for a moment, so far as we can tell from his writings, believed that he had abandoned his rabbinate, speaking always of himself as a Jew, "circumcised on the eighth day, of the people of Israel, of the tribe of Benjamin, a Hebrew born of Hebrews." He no more meant to found a new religion than good John Wesley (dying a faithful son of the Church of England) meant to found Methodism as a separate institution; or than Bishop Jansen intended to start the Jansenistic heresy which divided France in the eighteenth century. His fiery mission was announcing the glad tidings he himself had heard, and to announce them not only to the people of his own faith but to all the nations of the earth.

Poor Paul. The beginnings of his apostleship were hard. The Disciples suspected his sincerity, as well they might. The orthodox were shocked and intent on doing away with this dangerous renegade. Every man's hand seemed against him and he fled Damascus by having himself lowered over the wall in a basket—an action he looked back on later as a weakness in himself. But the Promise was stronger than his fears and on he went, frail, scrawny, indomitable; often ill, frequently beaten or flogged, shipwrecked, "once stoned," carrying the good news (which is literally what Gospel means) to any heart that would listen. He must have walked thousands of miles, since his pastorate reached from Caesarea to Rome, everywhere along the Aegean and Mediterranean seas as far as Malta and back again to Jerusalem. And during those twenty years or so of journeying, earning his living as he went, proselyting and building and teaching, he still managed to write the famous Epistles, of which we probably possess only a sampling.

But what a magnificent sampling they are! Fierce, touching, dogmatic by turns, they shaped Christian dogma and shaped also the world's thinking. If he had never written another text than the sublime one on love—or "charity" if you prefer—we would still have had a legacy to conjure with.

Those who call him puritanical seem to me wrong. For his age and upbringing—and in view of the congregations whom he variously addressed—he was vastly tolerant. When he spoke of subduing the flesh he may sound like the old hermits of Alexandria but he was no Manichee. To Paul the body was not evil as such. But to use it against itself and against virtue was to deny the Promise. Moreover there may have been odd practices creeping into some of his little foundations where converted pagans outnumbered the Hebrews. (Other saints have also had difficulty transplanting the faith in such soil and have been far harsher.) Some of his new adherents may once have been followers of Mithras or else of exceedingly permissive gods. With Paul's back turned, some of the overenthusiastic may have considered themselves dispensed from ordinary morality, a curious and prevalent outgrowth of many budding sects. There may have been sexual promiscuity, peculiar rites, profanation of the Feast. What seems to me remarkable is not that he was so stern but that he was so fatherly, eternally following some tirade, no doubt well-deserved, with words of compassion and of love. To some formerly Greek congregations where even respect for the old gods had grown limp, whom the strict morality of Judaism had never touched, he may have had to teach not only the simple elements of monotheism but monogamy too. No wonder so many of the letters deal with correct domestic behavior.

As for the Jewish converts, they were a different problem. He had to wean them away from so rigid an interpretation of the Mosaic law that it interfered with their full acceptance of other newly baptized comrades. Circumcision, for instance, was one of the points hotly debated by congregations. Even the Disciples split their ranks on the matter. Ought not all converts from *any* faith conform to the ancient Jewish custom? Paul fought for the liberty of choice on the part of Gentiles. The old law, he felt, has been superseded by the new enlightenment. Backed by a reluctant Peter, Paul carried the day. "Circumcision is nothing and uncircumcision is nothing," (but only) "the keeping of the commandments of God," he writes. And in Galatians we find him scandalized that any Apostle should fear to eat with the uncircumcised—which, of course, also meant eating out of dishes which were not ritually blessed. It was Paul's triumph that he perceived better than any other of his day the universality of the Message he had received on the road. Nothing counted except that Gospel. "For I through the law am dead to the law, that I might live unto God," he says exultingly. He had taken a gigantic step from the times when he had rejoiced in the stoning of a heretic.

Nor does he seem to me intolerant when he gives counsel on marriage, not even when he suggests in that often-disputed passage from Corinthians that "I would that all men were even as I myself"—which means celibate. What we must keep in mind is that Paul believed the second coming was very near. The Kingdom of this world was about to pass away. Why, then, should the unmarried bother to encumber themselves with a family when the matter at hand was to prepare their souls for that coming? "But this I say, brethren, the time is short," he writes an unruly congregation. Yet he understands the humanity of humankind. "It is better to marry than burn" has a surly sound. It is nothing of the sort. Those who find celibacy not within their powers had better marry and be done with yearning. There is nothing wrong with marriage except that it divides the attention and expends in public busyness that time which might be spent on meditation or private devotion. And then he goes on to say with tenderness, "Every man hath his proper gift of God, one after this manner, and another after that." He knows he is merely one example of a traveler on the Way.

And he is affectionate toward the married, begging them keep their state with love; saying that not even obdurate paganism on the part of one partner is sufficient to loosen the bond. Advice of that sort from so dedicated a bachelor seems to me broad-minded as charity itself.

"But what about this moralizing on the subservience of woman to her husband?" asks the outraged feminine contingent of his detractors. "What about the man being the head 'even as Christ is the head of the church'? What, particularly, about the injunction that women cover their heads and remain silent in the churches? Has it not been such Pauline teaching which kept women in purdah for so many centuries?"

What his opponents forget is that Paul was a first-century man, not an Ashley Montagu arguing the superiority of the feminine gender. Rather than lowering the position of women of his time, he elevated it. Among the citizens of such towns as Antioch and Corinth and Philippi, for instance, the Greek idea of marriage must have obtained—where the wife was of little account, divorce was easy, and husbands sought their diversion not at home but among the local Aspasias or Alcibiades'. Paul taught the vastly more dignified Jewish ideal of a proper family life where, if the husband was master and provider, the wife was to be cherished and eternally respected, a person not a chattel. "Let the husband render unto the wife due benevolence," he writes; and then (as I have already noted) he adds with decided firmness, "If any brother hath a wife that believeth not, and she be pleased to dwell with him, let him not put her away." One can imagine him in this passage answering the question of some too enthusiastic new Christian whose spouse obstinately refuses to join his devotions: "My wife is an unbeliever. Can't I send her back to her people?"

No one reading such a statement can maintain that
Paul was a misogamist—or a misogynist either. And
among the most touching of his personal notes, tucked
away at the end of his epistles, are the references to many
women who have rendered him kindnesses. "I commend
unto you Phebe, our sister," he says. Or "Greet Mary, who
bestowed much labor on us." Or again, "Salute . . . Julia,
Nereus, and his sister." Beneath the shifting translations
one can still hear the authentic voice of gratitude to the
good women of his far-flung parishes who, no doubt, not
only believed his message but also saw to it that when he
returned from his wanderings he had waiting for him clean
sheets and a hot dinner.

As for the rest of the rigid-sounding advice about
women covering their heads and holding their tongues in
church, the first is no more than good sense and the
second understandable. Respectable women *all* went
covered in those days and Paul wanted no irresponsible
behavior among his flock to scandalize the communities
where he was trying to build his enclaves of the faithful.
To attend services bareheaded was then rather as if one
would now go to church in a bikini. I don't suppose for a
minute that he thought a bareheaded woman would lose
her soul. But she *might* lose her reputation and it would
be fodder for the flames of gossip which always quickly
ignite about any young religion.

Paul grew practical as he grew wise and weather-
hardened. It must perpetually have tried his patience to
be forever settling such minor disputes when heart, mind,
and spirit wanted only to pass on the Word. Yet humanity
remained humanity even when banded together in the
new dispensation; and, like many another missionary after
him, he had to carry about with him the burden of the
world as it existed.

His admonition against women's being vocal in the
churches had a different origin. Wearing a veil was
merely conforming to decency of dress. But his insistence
that women keep silent at the commemorative supper was

something else again—a warning against hysteria. Once more, we must remember that these early Christians were human, and that they were enthusiasts. It is not improbable that the feverish atmosphere of a revival meeting often surrounded their services. Churches had sprung up everywhere along the Aegean but there was no Church as such, no written body of doctrine, no Bible, no disciplinary tradition. They had only the Word and the Feast, and most commentators admit that the feast now and then degenerated into an orgy of prophesying and "speaking with tongues." From what we know of the furor engendered even today by tent preachers and revivalists, the rolling in the aisles, the shouting and the singing and the uproar, it is not hard to imagine similar manifestations among Paul's flock when he was absent. We know, too, that women are most apt to be carried away in such circumstances. Perhaps there had been so much oracular behavior among them that the elders were worried. Paul did not particularly approve of prophecy even though it was in the Hebrew tradition. With the Messiah already come, what need had believers for personal visions? Moreover, on the practical side, women who abandoned dignity and turned themselves into shrieking furies lent ammunition to already hostile communities in which the church dwelt. Therefore let the ladies hold their tongues, conduct themselves with decorum, and maintain the peace which was part of the Revelation.

He might say as he did to the Galatians, "There is neither Jew nor Greek, there is neither male nor female; for ye are all . . . heirs according to the promise." But they were prospective heirs only, not yet come into that inheritance when the world would dissolve around them. Like his Master before him, he insisted they must render unto Caesar the things that were Caesar's; and if that meant obeying both civil and moral law and conforming as nearly as possible to local custom, then that was their patent duty.

He reminds them over and over that they are still

mortals, not disembodied spirits. They must continue to
follow their various trades, look after their children and
the home. He is very cross with the idealists who mis-
takenly think that because of the Promise they ought to
leave off all work and sit passively waiting for the heavens
to open and transport them into immediate paradise. Such
literal-minded members simply become a burden on more
industrious Christians, and he corrects them.

Indeed, considering the amount of correction he had to
produce in all his Epistles, it is miraculous that so much
is left of the tolerance and the glory.

All things to all men? What is hypocritical about such
an admission? It seems to me one of the grandest of his
statements, pure testimony of his large-heartedness. One
has continually to recall that Paul had been brought up
a Pharisee, taught to avoid the society of any but his own
cult. Yet he made himself for charity into a consorter
with men—and women—of all nationalities, all occupations,
all religions. Usurers or landowners, prostitutes or respectable matrons, soldiers, fishermen, the rich, the poor, the
illiterate or the governors of the land—in each of them
Paul saw not position but possibility. They were all his
brothers and his sisters. He was the first saint in the true
sense if one excludes martyrs—as I have done since a
daughter of mine once explained, "It's easy to be a
martyr. You only have to be it once." Paul may have become even a martyr at last, since it is believed that he
was beheaded under Nero. But his greatness lies not in
that but in his nobility of mind, soul, and intellect—and,
I repeat, in his enormous tolerance. He did love his neighbor as himself and with all the passion of a passionate
nature. Correction and scolding do not deny love; they
are the prerogative of the consistent lover.

And if he had written no other precept (although the
Epistles are so studded with exquisite ones that to read
Paul affectionately is to be eternally moved), there would
still remain the most superb passage in literature, the
magnificent if familiar thirteenth chapter of Corinthians.

Charity is love but it is love sublimated and made divine; it "beareth all things, believeth all things, hopeth all things, endureth all things."

Those lines are his signature. And they have become the first and last canon of holiness which every saint has followed, even if falteringly.

❀

Aspects of Sanctity

The Quality of Mercy

We live in the century of the Appeal. Organized charity thrives like the green bay tree and affects all our lives and purses. No mail comes to the door without its entreaty. The voice on the phone which interrupts our evening is likely to be that of yet another pleader for yet another mercy-distributing group.

One applauds the industry of professional philanthropy. But it has its dangers. After a while the private heart begins to harden. We fling letters into the wastebasket, are abrupt to telephoned solicitations. Charity withers in the incessant gale. It takes a saint to cope with such an excess of opportunity. And when I find my ears growing deaf, my eyes blind, toward Good Causes, that is exactly what I do—I take a saint or two from my library shelves. Reading their heroic lives, so full of absurd, soul-lifting generosity, I feel my sympathies for the distressed of the world re-engaged.

For saints, as one meets them in the Christian Calendar, come in an astonishing variety of shapes, sizes, and casts of mind. But I have never encountered a stingy one. From Martin, dividing his cloak with a stranger, to Katharine Drexel, lavishing her inheritance on neglected Indian children of our own era, they keep nothing, save nothing for themselves while any creature goes in want.

Mother Drexel is not yet officially a saint, although her admirers wait hopefully for Rome to take notice of her very American brand of holiness. But she deserves to be included among the blessed as much for stamina as for kindness. She *existed* for the sake of doing good—and I mean "existed" in its literal sense. Her father, one of the affluent Philadelphia Drexels, left her a fortune but he left it with strings attached. Since he approved neither her religious vocation nor her work among the non-Caucasian poor, his will stipulated that she could use only interest on the fortune, not capital; everything was to return to the estate on her death. Mother Drexel was a firm-minded woman and she needed that money for her charities. She set out obstinately to live as long as possible. When she died in her nineties scarcely more than a decade ago the family wealth had been used for more than seventy years, poured out for the benefit of Indians and Negroes displaced in their own country, spent on hospitals, schools, orphanages. Never underestimate the stubbornness of a woman or a saint.

Katharine Drexel belonged to our publicity-conscious age and she no doubt understood and bore with the charity which works by committee. What earlier saints would have made of our Community Chests and Red Cross drives one can merely conjecture. Francis of Assisi might have been merely bewildered, since he distrusted the good faith of large organizations, including that of his own Church. But many would have liked any act, no matter how impersonal, which helped a human being. For that matter, Vincent de Paul, patron of all charity, became in his lifetime a one-man relief agency, gathering about him all the open-hearted of France into ministering groups. Foundlings, prostitutes, galley slaves—the hungry, the crippled, the homeless, the rejected—they were all his children, and he prodded an entire nation into a frenzy of kindness for them. Yet even he would not have been content to let a salaried promoter come between him and the objects of his compassion. He would have scorned our calculated giving, which considers duty done when we have drawn a tax-deductible check for the United Hospital Appeal or bundled up our old winter coats for refugees (having, perhaps, first snipped off the fur collars).

Saints hated doing things by halves. They were of one mind with Richard of Wyche, medieval bishop, who, when his steward complained that the episcopal alms exceeded income, merely shrugged. "This place is full of the King's riches," he said. "Sell the gold dishes. Sell the carpets and the furniture." Then he added, making for an Englishman the supreme sacrifice, "And while you're about it, sell my horse."

Richard, like Robert Bellarmine in another land and another century, seems benevolent beyond the call of even saintly duty. Although Robert was forced to be a cardinal and live in a cardinal's palace, he lived there like a pauper, eating chiefly bread and garlic, "the food of the poor," and doing without fires for the sake of giving away what food and fires would cost. When he had got rid of everything worth pawning, including his ink pot, he pulled down the red wool curtains and had them made into clothes for shivering men. "The walls," he commented, "won't catch cold!"

Bellarmine seems on many counts a delightful character. He was a tiny man, so small he had to stand on a stool in the pulpit, but so persuasive that under his spell self-indulgent Italy reformed its ways. Galileo was his close friend and dedicated one of his books to him. The famous Recantation might never have come about if the scientist had listened to Robert's tactful advice. "Have a little prudence for the time being," he told Galileo. "Theologians are touchy these days—sore from the stings of a thousand wasps of heresy. They won't take kindly to what they may think is another dangerous novelty. Put out the book as theory; let truth prove it fact."

Galileo ignored counsel, and the resulting episode goes echoing down the years with his rebellious "Yet it does move" lingering on to rejoice skeptics and embarrass established religion.

Robert was as charitable in speech as in action. Although he launched his superb sermons against what he and the age considered heresy, he never mentioned his opponents by name for fear he might be guilty of detraction.

Detraction, by the way, is the most genial of sins. The act of making public some private lapse is what keeps columnists solvent, locker rooms agog, and dinner parties from collapsing into tedium. I suppose it is only enlarged gossip but it runs against charity all the same. Bellarmine hated it as did Hugh, Abbot of Grenoble, who so disliked to think ill of a friend that he refused to make out official reports. "Why should I set down faults?" he asked his baffled superiors.

Hugh, who in time of famine sold the chalice off his altar, is blood brother to Antoninus, famous today chiefly because his best friend was Fra Angelico. The latter angelic painter was so loved by the Florentines that they were about to make him a bishop by force. Antoninus did not relish the post either, but if it had to be a choice between him and the artist he knew his duty. So he left his meditations for an administrative life and Fra Angelico was allowed to go on contentedly covering monastery walls with his enchanting frescoes. The hands of Antoninus kept as busy with good deeds as did Angelico's with his brushes. During Italy's great earthquake in 1453, Antoninus followed the familiar saintly course, stripping all the churches and convents of their salable possessions down to the last cup and saucer for the relief of the homeless. He did something even more charitable; once the emergency was over he did not stop his care for the earthquake victims but helped them set up housekeeping again in decency when the rest of the city had forgotten them.

To give was the saints' passion. If they had money available, they spent that. If they were needy themselves, they begged for others as did Francis and his friend,

Saint Dominic, founder of the Dominican Order. (Demure little apostle that he was, Dominic comes off best for me with his human confession that he feared he "had taken more pleasure in the conversation of young women than of old.") Dominic kept himself in such a state of happy poverty that he died "in Brother Moneta's bed because he had none of his own; in Brother Moneta's habit because he had not another to replace the one he had so long been wearing."

I have run across an Ivo of Kermartin—a lawyer, of all things—who, when he discovered that a shelterless derelict had spent the night on his doorstep, brought the man into his own bed the next night while he occupied the doorstep himself.

One of the Desert Fathers had for his whole fortune a single codex of the Gospels, which he sold to feed the hungry. It was a gesture too daring for his friends to understand, books then being nearly as rare as unicorns. They accused him of sacrilege. "I sold only the Word," he told them, "which ever said to me, 'Sell what thou hast and give to the poor.'"

Such men belonged to eras when the public conscience had not yet been notably awakened to social wrongs. The poor walked the roads of the world depending for charity on the whims of the rich or the bounty of saints. Yet one of the most incorrigibly generous men who ever drew breath, Pius X, belongs to the comfortable and philanthropic nineteenth century. He was the despair of his relatives, his curates, and, in time, of the Vatican. When he was a priest in an Italian village, he seldom had a coat, since he was always running across a coatless parishioner; and he gave away even his socks, insisting to his scandalized sister who kept house for him, "It doesn't matter. The cassock covers everything."

He gave away the small fees he earned for his sermons, the firewood from his grate, the horse and cart he used for parish errands. One afternoon his sister came into the kitchen to stir the stew she had put on the stove for their

dinner. She was feeling rather pleased with herself for
having saved up enough *lire* to buy a little veal, meat
being rare in that house. Spoon in hand, she lifted up the
lid. Then, as she had every right to do, she burst into tears;
the dinner was gone. When she went wailing to her
brother, he patted her shoulder and said apologetically,
"What could I do? A hungry man knocked and I hadn't
anything else for him."

Alarmed authorities finally sent him to teach for a while
in a seminary for fear he would starve himself to death.
They managed to make him eat his meals, but they could
not cope with his prodigality. All his salary went for warm
clothes and treats for seminarians from poor families. In
spite of that and in spite of himself he was made a canon,
then a bishop, finally Pope. But no office could overwhelm
him (even the jewels in his official cross and ring were
replaced by paste), and he merely continued to be
generous on a larger scale. Since he ended his reign by
getting rid of the Church's material possessions in France,
he must have been well satisfied.

It is a good thing, I have often thought, that most of the
saints were celibate. Wives and children, bound to the
wheel of such extravagant impulses, might have been
hard put to it to defend themselves.

History leaves out the complaints of relatives except in
a case or two like that of Gummarus, whose feast is kept
rather obscurely in October. Gummarus had the bad
luck to be married to a wife so niggardly that while he
was away from home with King Pepin she refused the
harvesters their proper ration of beer. The biographer who
records this seems more aghast at the breach of hospitality than at the vixenish behavior which finally pushed
poor Gummarus into ending his days in a monastery. In
the eighth century beer was the great perquisite of the
working man; and one finds another saint, the Irish monk
Ceowulf, commended in the stories because he persuaded
his abbot to allow the monks—accustomed to drinking

only water—to "take a little beer or even wine" after their day in the fields.

Such modest charities warm me as much as the great ones. The mind can easily embrace them. For there are human needs as tormenting as lack of food or a roof, and the saints remembered those, too. **Hugh** of **Lincoln** brought the Carthusian Rule to **England** and defended English serfs against the inhumanity of three wily Plantagenet kings. But when he was a monk at the Grande Chartreuse and there were no alms left for the poor, he consoled them by "listening to their troubles."

Ethelbert of Kent, too, had his own kind of generosity. When he was converted from paganism he resisted the impulse of most converts to change the ways of everyone else, and he assured his people that they might remain pagan if they chose. Some of them did so, like the last heathen king of the Frisians, who said that while Christianity might be true and all that he preferred to be in hell with his ancestors rather than in heaven with strangers.

I love such eccentric blessings. Caesarius of Arles, a celebrated preacher, seems to me engaging because he limited his sermons to fifteen minutes, and Nicholas the Pilgrim because his pockets were always full of apples and candy for the children he met on his wanderings.

Juvenal Ancina invented his own odd method for restoring self-respect to down-and-outers. He kept a charge account at various barbers' where the proprietors had orders to invite into their shops any impoverished man they noticed in need of a haircut. "Don't let them know there's a benefactor," warned the saint earnestly. "Just put it all down to Brother Juvenal."

He understood how the spirit can fail when it must summon up too much gratitude. So, too, did Godfrey de la Haye, a good physician nicknamed Godfrey Zonderdonk, which means "Don't mention it." Godfrey got his title because when he treated the poor he refused to be thanked. "Please, please—don't mention it," he would beg them, recoiling from their thanks as impulsively as he was drawn to their wretchedness.

I like to read about the random generosity of Albinus, who helped poor widows struggling to bring up large families; or about civic-minded Edwin, the King who provided fountains and brass cups on medieval highways for the convenience of thirsty travelers. And I can be kindled into kindness by the strange charity of Thomas More, who, deciding to take a wife, looked with favor on the younger daughter of one house but married the elder because she might be ashamed to have her sister wed before her. (It is consoling to learn that the pair lived together very happily and that when she died More put up a stone with the single understated line, "To the memory of my little wife, Jane.")

One saint, finally, remains to comfort those of us who find our purse strings tightening or our hearts constricting under an avalanche of solicitations. Her name is Joan Delanoue, and she is the exception which maintains the rule that no saint is avaricious. For Joan began her career as a miser. Her father had been a small merchant at Saumur in the French province of Anjou, dealing in cloth, crockery, and religious trinkets to suit the taste of pilgrims to a nearby shrine. When he died he left her a house and the shop and Joan settled down to making a good thing out of trade. She bought cheap, sold dear, and gave no credit. The store was open seven days a week, to the scandal of the parish. And as a sideline she crowded belated pilgrims into her house for an exorbitant nightly fee.

What changed her nature it is difficult to say. But saints have recovered from more picturesque depravities than stinginess and Joan did at length repent. She began in a small way by giving away one of her dresses. It was her first draught of the wine of charity, and evidently an intoxicating one. It went straight to her heart. Before long, like an addict, she was tippling in secret—taking clothes from the closet to hand out after dark to the unfortunate, opening her purse to any case of need. Tramps found a meal with her, the insolvent could run up bills. As her income dwindled her mercies expanded. Soon she was looking after several orphans in her little house and taking in off the street anyone who seemed destitute. When the shop failed from too much giving, she went out to work for her guests if she could find work, to wheedle from the rich if she could not. At last she gathered about her several women with hearts nearly as large as hers had grown, and together they founded a sanctuary called Great Providence House, which cared for all the wretched of Saumur—and does so to this day.

In our welfare society there seems less and less need for the Joans, or the Vincent de Pauls, taking on single-handed the miseries of a town or a nation. It is the great accomplishment of our time that alms as medieval saints understood them are nearly out of date. The poor and the old have state pensions. The sick have a place to turn and a hand to reach for even when it is only a cold public hand. But there are still a thousand lacks and wants.

When we separate ourselves from them, when we make do with a check or our cast-off clothing, a certain brightness falls from the air. To know the joy of charity we must experience the actual pinch of giving—of giving our time to hospitals, our skills to helping the illiterate to read or the crippled to walk, our abilities to comforting those in need of comfort. We are a generous nation, and any emergency brings out the best in us, but there are chronic small distresses which sometimes only an underpaid and overworked social agent ever sees; there are always deprived children, the friendless old. There are still prisons and foundling homes and inadequate nursing staffs and schools begging for amateur aids. Perhaps giving our strength is beyond our capacities. Then charity might consist for us merely in writing a letter which we have put off, or listening, like Hugh, to people's troubles. So long as it is a personal act, we share the saints' great secret.

Ascent from Grandeur

Behaviorists, these days, preach the doctrine that we are all victims immutably shaped either by our genes or by our environment. Free will, as a phrase, carries with it too much sentiment, too metaphysical a content, to be accepted by our pessimistic generation. Yet it is a concept to which romantics like me continue to cling. I have spied too long on Christian saints—and non-Christian ones, as well—to feel that man is, like the lesser animals, unable to reverse his nature.

The calendar is full of sinners converted to sanctity. Joan the miser becomes Joan the spendthrift for charity. Ubald of Florence leads until he is thirty "a turbulent life with dissipated companions," then makes the rest of his long existence a poem of gentleness and piety. Or Pelagia, the notorious Harlot of Antioch, equally celebrated as Butler primly puts it "for her beauty and disorder of her life," becomes Pelagia the famous penitent, giving to the poor, as a first gesture of remorse, her priceless collection of pearls, each donated by one of her various lovers.

Such conduct rings outrageously on modern ears and is quite easily explained away by references to hysteria. And it is perfectly true that extravagant vice often leads to theatrical repentance. The passionate nature remains passionate even when directed toward an altered goal.

Pelagia might fit nicely nowadays into a literature which specializes in the theme of salvation through sin. But we ordinary aspirers need another sort of path to follow, some patient, plodding route open to the pedestrian traveler. We distrust as beyond our abilities the pole vault from depths to seraphic height.

Among the plodders I have a favorite. He is not so well known as his accomplishments deserve but his story always refreshes me. For in his person he refutes both those who rely on inheritance and those who defend environment as single keys to behavior. In him free will reaches its apotheosis.

Not that he is humdrum or that the circumstances of his life are apt to match ours. On the contrary, his rearing and his origins are equally spectacular. His very surname sends shivers down the spine. For he is Saint Francis Borgia, majestic grandee of sixteenth-century Spain, cousin to the Emperor. Only in his long and clumsy ascent from the rags of temporal glory to the riches of the spirit do his adventures touch on our small clamberings.

Poor man, what Alps he had to scale! The *Catholic Encyclopedia* describes him as "unfortunate in his ancestry"—hilarious understatement even for that sober tome. A true behaviorist might consider him doomed from birth. For in his veins (although chiefly illegitimately) ran the grandest, the cruelest, the most vicious blood of Europe. His mother's grandfather was Ferdinand of Aragon, whose claim to renown is that while he was ruthlessly uniting Spain into an empire he was just as ruthlessly driving out the Moors from Granada and the Jews from the whole kingdom. Ferdinand cannot even be credited with sponsoring Columbus, since he at first opposed Isabella's patronage of that persevering admiral when he set out to prove the world was round.

On his father's side, Francis had to claim as ancestor Alexander VI, a Borgia and the wickedest pope who ever bought, bribed, and threatened his way to the tiara.

Much has been written about the Borgias. They have

become legend, metaphors for evil, so picturesque in their
ill-doings that some cynics profess to admire them. But
most of us know only vaguely their place in Spanish and
Roman history.

Actually they were not Italians at all but Spanish minor
aristocrats, adventurers and opportunists to a man. Rome,
however, was the site of their best-recorded iniquities.
They began their unspeakable activities there by accident.
In 1455 they happened to have as head of the family a
certain Cardinal Alonzo who was unexpectedly elected
pope and took the name Callixtus III. Like the late John
XXIII he took office as an "interim" pontiff (all other
balloting having failed to bring a majority) and also like
him he had an effect on the Papacy far beyond anyone's
imaginings. I add hastily that in no other way did he re-
semble the redoubtable John.

Callixtus seems to have been a fairly innocuous old
fellow as popes went in those confused days. At least he
was said to have been "true to his word" and inoffensive
as far as his personal morality was concerned. To an on-
looker, however, he seems belligerent rather than kind.
During his brief reign (he was eighty when he came to
office and died in 1458) he assiduously denounced the
Turks and would have fought a crusade if anybody had
been willing to listen to him. He also sold or gave away
as frivolous the handsome library amassed by his pred-
ecessor, the humanist Pope Nicholas V. The most I can
find to his credit is his rehabilitation of Joan of Arc, whom
he absolved posthumously from taint of sin or heresy—
not much comfort to Joan but some solace, one supposes,
to her relatives.

But if he did no particular evil, he gave rise to it. For
what he owned to the point of mania was family pride.
To Rome he fetched his brothers, nephews, cousins; and
he showered on them every gift in his possession. He gave
them fiefs, titles, ecclesiastical honors. His particular pet
was a twenty-six-year-old swashbuckling nephew named
Rodrigo, whom he first made a cardinal and then vice-

chancellor of the Church, an office second to that of pope. Rodrigo, after having fathered four children out of wedlock—Peter, Lucretia, Juan, and the infamous Caesar—eventually became Pope Alexander VI and through his second son, Juan, ancestor to Francis.

Catholics have long treasured an intramural joke about the divinity of the Church. The proof, they insist, lies in the fact that it has lasted nearly two thousand years "in spite of the clergy." Certainly the lives of such men as Alexander foster the jest. He was not only a creature of his age and country but also a begetter. The tides of the Renaissance were beating against the shores of Mediterranean Europe. Yet while they washed away ignorance they likewise were destroying innocence, leaving worldliness like silt upon religion. Rome, of all cities, suffered most. It was not even prosperous as were Florence, Ferrara, and Venice, but decadent, nearly a ruin. Its inhabitants, says Compano, a contemporary poet, "are more like barbarians than Romans; they are repellent of aspect and speak the most differing dialects; they are unruly and lacking in education. Even the bourgeois . . . are dedicated to an effeminate life of pleasure, pride, and wantonness."

Under Alexander this wantonness enlarged itself. Clerical abuses became so common that it was a rare bishop who did not sell his benefices, and a peculiar priest who kept no concubine.

Reforming voices rose as they always do. Some record of those voices still exists—the words of good men sorrowing over the plight of their world. "We are rushing headlong to disaster," cried Brandolini Lippo, the blind preacher. "I despair not only of our earthly life but of our eternal salvation, so debased is our moral and social life by those who should improve and sustain it. Virgins are raped and the mothers of families are prostituted; sacred properties appropriated by corrupt means and houses plundered; people are thrown in the Tiber and murder is committed with impunity by day and night."

But the voices were either ignored or, like Savonarola's, silenced by death. There existed no Italian Luther to nail his theses to a church door or any monarch strong enough to rebuild the Papacy by might of arms; for the Borgias, in spite of their immorality, were not stupid. They were handsome, suave, brilliant, and cunning, quite able to outwit their enemies. Before he purchased his popedom, Alexander had, as a cardinal, attained enormous wealth and power. After his rigged election he continued to consolidate those gains by any means that came to hand —lies, treachery, assassination. Nor did he attempt to veil his lechery. He was not the first pope to flaunt his bastards; Innocent VIII had done it before him. But Alexander went that misnamed prelate one better. He got them legitimatized by special writ so that they could make what he considered suitable marriages.

Hapless Lucretia he married off five times before she was twenty-three, each time to a grander husband, for his own political gain. Her first marriage he took the trouble to have annulled on the spurious grounds of impotence. Her other husbands either caught the signal and fled or stayed and were murdered. Biographers of that day contend that before she was wedded at all she had been debauched by both her father and her brother, Caesar; but there is no final proof and Rome of that era so hated all Borgias that they would believe any evil rumor concerning them.

To his son, Peter, Alexander gave the Duchy of Gandia in Spain. When Peter died, the next and then favorite son, Juan, became Duke. Juan was murdered by Caesar, some say for envy over Gandia, others claim out of incestuous love for Lucretia. Before he died, however, Juan did produce an heir, also named Juan, who succeeded to the dukedom, married the daughter of a natural son of Ferdinand, and had an heir of his own. That son was Francis, who against all probabilities became the saint of the clan.

By the time of his birth in 1510 the Italian Borgias

were in eclipse, their reign of terror ended by Alexander's death (appropriately by poison) and Caesar's subsequent overthrow. The despised Pope finished his days almost as monstrously as he had lived them. Before he had even stopped breathing his guards and servants decamped, taking in their flight whatever of his portable possessions they could lay hands on. The coffin hastily run up for him was too small and his decaying corpse was squeezed and crushed into it by undertakers who "all amused themselves and indulged in buffoonery" around the bier. A commentator of the period writes this hate-drenched paragraph: "All the people of Rome flocked with extraordinary gladness to see Alexander's body in Saint Peter's, unable to content their eyes with the sight of the dead serpent who, with excessive ambition and foul treachery, with every kind of terrible cruelty . . . lechery and unheard-of greed, indiscriminately selling things sacred and profane, had infected the whole world."

In Spain, however, the house of Gandia had suffered no decline. On the contrary, alliance to the royal family, even if on the left-hand side, made for a glittering court. Gandia was an important province of the Spanish Empire and the empire was the most prosperous in Europe. Riches poured from the colonies, from Goa, from the Americas both North and South, as from a bottomless cornucopia. And Francis was a part of all this, not only the Emperor's cousin but his confidant, a courtier genial and magnificent, talked of as future minister of state.

That Francis was a Borgia mutation one must grant. In later life he spoke of himself as a tremendous sinner, but the histories do not vindicate his confession. However, he no more wore a halo from childhood than did any of my other heroes. "The phenomenon of holiness so near the grandest of European thrones," writes James Brodrick, "dazzled the biographers. They made him a saint from his cradle, whereas he won his spiritual spurs in battle, like a soldier. They turned him into a dull legend, a stiff, thin-lipped, brocaded saint, vice-regal even when he

scourged himself, whereas, in fact, the only evidence of
high if crooked lineage that clung to him was an exquisite
courtesy of demeanour."

There was, in other words, nothing miraculous about
him except his steady climbing. That and the fact he chose
to climb at all. For his upbringing was as unpromising as
his ancestry. He was sent as a child to Saragossa to get
his education at the court of his maternal uncle, the
Archbishop—"an ostentatious prelate," says the *Catholic
Encyclopedia,* "who had never been consecrated nor even
ordained a priest." One can picture the sort of tutelage
Francis received there—Latin and laxity; appreciation of
music and a sense of his own importance; stuffy pomp
and hollow piety. And if Saragossa were not enough to
stifle his natural mercies, the succeeding environment
should have accomplished it. For he went at twelve to
Aragon as page to the Infanta. For five years he shuttled
back and forth between the two grandiose palaces until he
was considered a fully fledged grandee, ready to ornament
the court of the Emperor Charles.

Ornament it he did, so the histories say. He rose from
post to worldly post, became Viceroy of Catalonia, and
was finally slated, as I have mentioned, to be future
chancellor of the kingdom. Then something happened to
him which may have seemed at the time a setback but
which, if one considers sainthood a goal worth striving
for, perhaps turned him toward something better than
even his admirers could have planned for him. Charles'
son, Philip, was about to marry the Princess of Portugal
and Francis was named master of their household. Portugal
opposed the appointment. Perhaps they feared Francis
would stand in the way of planned machinations; for already the saint-to-be was earning, along with public renown, a reputation for honorable conduct and piety unusual in a layman. In fact it was scandalous, people
whispered, how attentive he was at church and how frequently he took the sacraments. At any rate, he was refused the office. So on his father's death, Francis returned

to Gandia. Who are we to know whether or not he went
with as much relief as disappointment?

The one useful talent handed down to him by the
Borgias was a gift for administration. In Gandia he set
about immediately to improve the province's affairs. He
repaired hospitals, built schools, fortified the duchy
against raiding Barbary pirates, and made sure his people
were prosperous. He is also said to have taken personal
charge of seeing that robbers and bandits vanished from
his borders. He used to ride boldly after them into the
hills and, having overtaken them, hanged them on the
spot. It must have been a mighty horse that carried him,
for he was an immense man. "Portly" is the pleasantest
adjective one can use in describing his girth. Pious paint-
ings made after his canonization depict him as lean and
ascetic, "a bag of bones," and he did toward the end of
his life subdue his weight by dint of work and fastings.
But for many years he was so huge that, like Thomas
Aquinas, he had to have half-moons cut out of desks and
tables so he could fit into them; and his belt "would go
around three normally proportioned people." Yet if his
plumpness was noticeable, so was his kindness.

The poor and the ignorant were his special concern.
For the yeast of sanctity was stirring in him even then,
and if his compassion did not extend to bandits, it did
reach to every man of good will. No leaning toward vice
made his climb to heaven difficult. What impeded him,
dragged at his heels, was what in a lesser degree slows
down us all—comfort, success, domestic contentment. At
this stage Francis seems on a large scale the image of a
benign and bustling country squire, scurrying about his
estates, looking after his tenants, improving his properties.
Even in an age of arranged marriages, he adored his wife.
He cherished his eight children and loved, along with the
pleasures of table and the hunt, books, music, and his
friends. Where he differed from other beneficent landlords—and this was his snag on the Road—was his habit of
grandeur, his natural thirst for authority.

The Jesuits, whom he first protected and later led, suffered early from this trait. They were a very young order when Francis met them, a struggling little band of mendicants, vilified by older and more tradition-encrusted foundations and so suspect in Spain that bishops thundered from pulpits such as Toledo's against Ignatius Loyola, the "Anti-Christ." Francis, however, had met a few of the strange new priests when he was Viceroy of Catalonia and had been moved by their dedication and good works. (He could not have admired much else about them, since they were poorer than the poorest subjects in the realm, roving about preaching, teaching, living on alms, and bedding down in any hovel they could find.) He had even begun a correspondence with Ignatius that lasted all their lives and so initiated a friendship which Brodrick calls "love at first reading."

He picked on the Jesuits (and I intend the pun) to help him with his schools in Gandia. When seven of them finally arrived at his urging, he told them what was on his imperious mind. He wanted to found not only lower schools, not only a small college, but a university. The seven were in despair. Forty miles up the coast was the populous University of Valencia—how was little Gandia to compete with that institution? But Francis was so persuasive, and such patrons as he so uncommon, that the university got built and eventually staffed. It never became important, but the Jesuits were loyally keeping it going two centuries later. And while the Fathers toiled, Francis watched them, encouraged them, and began to pattern his interior life after them. Though still a duke rather than a saint, he was taking his early steps up the mountain.

He asked and received permission from Ignatius to attempt the Spiritual Exercises, those disciplined meditations which were and still are the peculiar stamp of the Jesuit Order. The great heart in that corpulent body was no longer yearning after worldly honors but only toward the God he had always taken seriously.

In 1546 real misfortune, to which he had seemed singularly immune, struck suddenly. His wife died, his beloved Eleanor. Sorrowing over her, he reached a decision: if Ignatius, the father-general, permitted it, he would himself become a Jesuit.

It was probably the one sensational gesture Francis ever made. For he was only thirty-seven, still young enough to expect a splendid future in Spanish government. All that splendor he was prepared to fling away to join an upstart, poverty-stricken order whose members were required by charter to promise they would accept no clerical honors—no bishopric, no cardinal's hat. It was almost as startling as if the Prince of Wales, today, were to join the Salvation Army. Indeed the idea, while it delighted Ignatius, also daunted him. He wrote, suggesting extreme caution, begging the Duke to make no such dramatic move until he had thought it over very cautiously. He reminded his patron that nothing could be arranged until Francis had settled the affairs of his children, provided his daughters with husbands, named his heir, given proper allowances to the younger sons, and himself gone back to school to study theology. He also implored the impetuous applicant not to let the news out prematurely. "The ears of the world," he explained, "are not ready for such an explosion."

Ignatius was a capable wheedler, remarkable for his combination of practicality and mysticism. His letter, which Francis obeyed, marked perhaps the first time the Duke had *had* to obey any command except the King's. That he took the delay so meekly shows how far he had already clambered.

Ignatius had planned that the noble candidate should wait in patience many months to profess himself a Jesuit. But when the following year Aragon summoned the Duke to its parliament, he relented. The world must not again capture this prize. So Francis was allowed in a private ceremony to become a novice. He spent the next three years securing the peace of Gandia, making over his title and estates to his son Charles, seeing to the needs of his other children, and enrolling at his own little university as its first pupil. By 1551 when he had just passed forty he was ordained a priest and entered the order's hermitage at Onate.

That ordination was the "explosion" Ignatius had prophesied. When Father Francis said his first Mass, attending crowds were so large that an altar had to be set up outdoors. A duke turned mendicant was not an everyday sight.

His brother Jesuits treated him with more rigor than did the populace. The superior at Onate was only human and may have taken a slightly malicious pleasure in making clear to Francis that he was no longer a Spanish peer, only a fledgling priest. So grandee became scullery boy, fetched wood and water, laid fires, and apologized to the company when he served them awkwardly at table.

I doubt this bothered Francis. New penitents welcome humiliation; and records show he took offense only when someone carelessly addressed him as "Your Grace." In truth, he made such heroic attempts at turning saint overnight that Ignatius had to warn him against practicing mortifications too severe. Francis always did things lavishly. Even before he signed away his duchy, he was giving more money to charity and disciplining his body more harshly than Ignatius (an old hand at guiding novices) thought reasonable. What perhaps the practical father-general forgot was that it was Borgia wealth and Borgia blood Francis was spilling in eternal expiation.

The severities, though, he imposed only on himself. With others he was all courtesy and charm. His nature never soured. As he grew in virtue he grew also in charity for mankind. And how it was needed in sixteenth-century Spain! Torquemada was dead but the Inquisition he had helped shape still followed his cruel design. The Spanish Church, the Spanish State, were one. Heresy was considered treason and no punishment too dreadful for dissenters. Francis fought the Inquisition as he had battled his own lineage, but with less success. As the Emperor's cousin he had influence still and he saved those he could. Those he could not rescue he followed to the foot of every cross. He himself was in constant danger. His opinions were disputed, his books were banned, and he was finally called to Rome in 1561 by superiors who feared for his safety.

There he overcame the last obstacles of his long upward journey. The Matterhorn was in sight, the rope stout; but there were still human faults opening like crevasses under his feet. These he had to skirt or leap across. Particularly, he had to unlearn certain disciplines. It had been a struggle for him to subdue his inheritance of natural authority. In his first years as a Jesuit, even while he was trying his best to be humble, he was apt to think up grandiose schemes for the Order and to issue them like fiats. Now that he had pretty will mastered this temptation, he was faced with its opposite. Now he truly wished to be an anonymous priest, perhaps a missioner to the Americas. But the Society, which has always valued talent, thought otherwise and decided to promote him. Since the good of the Order came first with him he put aside on command his ache for simplicity. When first Ignatius, then Laynez, valiant successor, both died at their desks, Francis accepted the generalship of the Society of Jesus. The list of his accomplishments during the seven years he served reads like a flourish of trumpets. He founded foreign missions, built seminaries and hospitals, helped expand and codify the Society's Rule. He worked unceasingly at reforming the Church itself; and by his enormous powers of persuasion helped make the Jesuits respectable in the eyes of popes and peoples. The present Gregorian College was endowed and invented by him although he refused to let his name be given it. He may, as Jesuit histories say, have roofed the house that Ignatius founded and Laynez walled. But those in a way were worldly triumphs, and Francis never let himself turn into a religious computer. Even at his busiest he remembered the individual charities which obsess a saint.

In Spain he had comforted people as well as groups, cheering melancholy novices, aiding the poor, lending his strong shoulder as prop for any weary man who wished to lean on him. He had been among the first to recognize the genius of Teresa of Avila and to encourage her along her angelic bent. His passion was to guide, counsel, console. Now in Rome he discontinued neither his hospitality nor his solacing. The whole city became his parish. Poverty, plague, ignorance, and despair—with all these he came personally to grips.

When he died in 1572 his name was a bouquet everywhere in Europe to those that loved the perfume of goodness.

His, I repeat, was not a romantic life in spite of works and lineage. His real adventures went on secretly, in the depths of his generous soul. Reading hagiography has nearly convinced me that it is easier for a flamboyant sinner to achieve heaven than for an ordinary virtuous, complacent man. Francis by free will managed everything—to attain sainthood in spite of ancestry, rearing, and born amiability. Nor did he ever freeze into a posture less than human.

"Indeed," says Brodrick, "not only was he human but a humanist, a saint in the line of Assisi's Francis who . . . loved everything beautiful that kept its innocence." Then Brodrick adds, in a requiem sentence better than any I could frame, "He was one of the sweetest, dearest, noblest men our poor old world has known."

On his deathbed Francis spoke the name of each of his children and blessed them. Perhaps he prayed also for the soul of Alexander.

Kind Men and Beasts

It is one of the ironies of this ironic age that man, so hard on his own kind, so ready to wipe out his own works and marvels, grows constantly more sympathetic toward his brothers, the beasts. In a century that contains Dachau and the hundred-megaton bomb we have invented vast game sanctuaries for elephants or warthogs and tirelessly protect the whooping crane. In my own village I am constrained by law from trapping the gray squirrel, which, with nothing in his favor except cheeky good looks, yearly raids my walnut tree and mutilates my attic. If so much as a sparrow falls, the Humane Society rushes a specialist to its rescue. Now that science has discovered the genial dolphin with its high I.Q. and plans to teach it to talk, the Peaceable Kingdom seems very near at hand. It is as if man and beast were preparing to lie down together in the teeth of the approaching storm, as lion and gazelle close ranks when a forest fire menaces or water holes run dry.

Consideration for animals is a singularly modern phenomenon. In earlier centuries, Saladin might love his charger or a medieval lady pamper her hound. But the general run of humanity thought their dumb brothers expendable, outside the fold of compassion. Only the Christian saints behaved differently—walked, as saints always do, ahead of their times. Long before Game Reservations or the S.P.C.A. were dreamed of, holy men were being tender in a less self-conscious way than we to everything that stirred in woods or jungles or the air.

Old tales are full of their mercies. A Saint Malo refuses to move his cloak because a wren is nesting in it. Columba of Iona nurses an exhausted crane blown off its course to his monastery, then after three days sets it free to return to the Ireland from which he is forever exiled. Godruc of Finchale—he who had been a pirate in his youth but who after a pilgrimage to Jerusalem made a vow to "put no shoes upon these feet" because Christ had been crucified barefoot—goes about shoeless in the winter frost "peering under hedges for such small animals as might be helpless with the cold."

Thomas Becket won a halo for getting himself murdered in a cathedral. But he has my personal salute because he taught the English to treat horses kindly. And Pius V, intimidating prelate though he might seem from this distance, when he was not busy trying to make a good Catholic out of the first Elizabeth or defending Europe from the Turks, was furiously proselyting against the sport of bullfights in Spain. Poor man! Evidently he understood neither the English nor the Spanish national character, for he was as unsuccessful with the one as with the other.

For two millennia, and long before it was fashionable, saints have been making friends of the beasts. It is one of the tenderest chapters in Christianity and not well enough remembered. I have already mentioned Francis of Assisi, who named the birds his sisters and cherished the mice tormenting him in his cell. Francis sometimes seems the only saint that people everywhere recognize and accept, if often for the wrong reasons. His statue, inane as a greeting card, stands in thousands of suburban gardens where he is halfway confused with Pan, or even Peter Pan. The real Francis, stern to himself, a preacher, an organizer, above all a reformer, is quite a different person from the meek little dreamer of legend. But of course part of the legendary Francis is real as myths always are. For Francis, like his Master, so loved the world that the meanest inhabitant in it called upon his pity.

Some of the stories about Francis may sound apocryphal, like the tale of the grasshopper which on a winter midnight came to help him sing his office, leaving its tiny tracks in the snow to shame monks who had been too slothful to assist. Still, his heart truly brimmed over with such affection it had to scatter like rain onto animals as well as men. He particularly loved the crested lark, dressed like a good religious in a brown habit and hood, and the story goes that on the evening of his death a cloud of larks wheeled over his house and grievingly sang their farewells. (An equally touching if even less likely story is told about Blessed Gandulf of Binasco, one of Francis's own friars. When Binasco's body was being enshrined, the swallows he had once scolded for chattering too loudly while he preached flew into the church during the night, then "parted into two groups and sang, in alternating choirs, a *Te Deum* of their own.")

The flight of Francis's larks may have been coincidence, yet they mourned with reason, since they were losing a great friend. He felt so strongly for the mistreated animals of his day, for the snared birds and beaten horses and hungry dogs, that he went to the burghers, to the governors, finally to the Emperor, begging for a law against their abuse. He demanded that farmers be forced to treat their cattle humanely and give them an extra treat on Christmas Day. He wanted towns and corporations to take time off from levying taxes and scatter crumbs, instead, on the frozen roads. He pleaded for hostels where strays could be fed and housed, and he raged against the caging of larks. Like his plan to stop the Crusades by a personal interview with the Sultan, these schemes came to little. But in Assisi to this day, at the time of the Angelus, they feed his birds in the market place.

There are a host of lesser Francises, however, affected like him (to quote the *Mirror of Perfection*) "with a singular and overflowing love toward creatures." In that love there is a remarkable lack of condescension. Few of the saints seem to have kept pets as such. They were too busy or too practical or too afraid of distraction on their lifelong journeys toward God. The *Ancren Rule*, an anonymous tract written in the thirteenth century for the instruction of ladies about to enter English convents, does, in fact, specifically discourage the custom of having dumb favorites and suggests only that the nuns "might keep a cat"; and today the convent cat is still rather an institution. But to saints animals were not poppets, only familiars, created things that must be helped or tended or disciplined as the occasion arose. They felt toward them as they would have felt toward any necessitous being in the universe.

Perhaps they bound up their wounds as Gerasimus the Abbot did for the lion he found limping along beside the river Jordan with a thorn in its paw. Or they fed them as Walaricus fed the birds which came tamely to be fed while he warned off intruding visitors with a gentle "Do let these innocents eat in peace." Walaricus lived peacefully as his thrushes, but he must have wrung his hands in heaven over what happened after his death. When William the Conqueror was about to set sail against England in 1066 he dug up the good man's body and exposed it publicly as a sort of ransom for a favorable wind. One is surprised that Walaricus did not send a tempest.

No matter how needy they were themselves, saints always managed for animals (as for the poor) food, nursing, and lodging for the night. Perhaps they sheltered them as Aldemar sheltered the bees which made a hive of one of the cupboards in his monastery without his having the heart to disturb them; or as Martin de Porres sheltered all waifs and strays. Martin is a kind of mulatto Saint Francis, one of the most charming characters in the calendar. He lived in Peru in the violent sixteenth century and in a violent land, the son of a Spanish knight and a colored freed woman, and was friend to a more typically Latin wonder worker, the celebrated Rose of Lima. Butler's *Lives of the Saints* explains that Brother Martin's charity "embraced the lower animals" which, the author interpolates, "surprised the Spaniards"; and that he treasured even the vermin which nibbled the monastery vestments, excusing the depredations of rats and mice on the ground that "the poor little things were insufficiently fed"—a saying which might have astonished anyone, since the creatures lived in his granaries. Martin constituted himself a one-man Humane Society and kept a hospital for dogs and cats at his sister's house. I suspect his sister deserves her nimbus too.

Or perhaps they went so far as to teach their charges good manners and how to behave like Christians—or rather as Christians were supposed to behave. William Firmatus, a French anchorite who lived in the eleventh century, was such an instructor. Kind old William had so great a power over animals that the peasants of his region used to appeal to him for protection for their fields and gardens. And it is said that "with a gentle tap he would admonish the hares and goats that frisked about him and the birds as they nestled for warmth in his habit." When gentleness got nowhere he took severer measures. The countryside was being ravaged by a wild boar, as happened frequently in the Brittany of 1090. William found the boar, took it firmly by one ear, led it to a cell, and shut it up there, bidding it "fast all night." And when he set it free in the morning, the beast was "cured forever of its marauding proclivities." Curing things was perhaps a natural talent of William's, since he had once been trained for a physician but amazingly enough forsook his vocation when he discovered in himself a leaning toward avarice!

The Godruc who went looking for small victims of the winter weather also had his tutorial side. Like any proper hermit, he was a great gardener and orchardman. When rabbits and roving herds of deer broke into his hermitage to nibble the young shoots of fruit trees or carry off the vegetables intended for the poor, he put up with it for a while until famine threatened. Then he scolded the hares, gave them a bundle of carrots, and told them to look for wilder forage. The deer he led into the forest, explaining that he meant his trees for humans, not animals; and the obedient deer bothered him no more. He even taught a surly bear which was stealing his honey that there were legal supplies outside in the woods and the bear, too, did as he was told "although with bad grace." Godruc, one feels, could have dealt with larcenous squirrels, and I wish I could call on his talents. In unforgiving moments I would be willing even to summon up a Saint Bernard to excommunicate them as he excommunicated the flies that pestered him and his congregation in the church at Foigny, "so that they all died."

Few saints, though, were so severe as Bernard. Francis of Paula spared the wasps in his garden as Joseph of Anchieta spared the vipers. Patrick, to be sure, cast the snakes out of Ireland. But the legend does not insist that he worked any harsher curse on them than exile to a better climate. And sometimes the dear old people sound more lenient than the most extravagant supporter of the S.P.C.A. Richard of Wyche was a great bishop, and so felt it his duty to be hospitable and give his guests meat for their meals. But he ate none himself and mourned when he saw lambs or chickens or ducklings being brought to the kitchen. "Poor things! You don't deserve to die," he said only half-humorously, sounding rather like a conscientious vegetarian of today. Philip Neri, who refused to *be* a bishop, was more consistent. The pheasants and pigeons that were sent to him as gifts for his table he returned with a polite note, begging the sender to keep the birds alive for him. Francis de Sales rescued a stag when it fled to him for refuge from the King's hunters, which is not extraordinary when one remembers that half of human France was in the habit of running to Francis for consolation.

It is cheering to read that so long ago as medieval days, when ordinary men, trying to save their bodies as well as their souls, were too harassed to worry about beasts, protectors rose in the land with laws and sanctuaries. Gilbert of Sempringham, the only Englishman who ever founded a lasting religious order, the Gilbertines, laid down rules for his domain. Anybody found mistreating any dumb creature there had to account for his sin to the charitable Gilbert. And Hugh of Lincoln in the time of Richard the Lion-Hearted, not content with charming kings and other sinners, made friends with a wild swan. Naturalists versed in the ways of swans will bend the knee before such a feat. A pair of them lord it over a certain millpond near where I live and I would as soon try to tame a tiger as those malicious birds. Wicked and beautiful, with their feathers like brush strokes in a Japanese painting, with their coral beaks and angry little eyes, they live in a state of perpetual self-invoked fury. They take less joy in gobbling up the bread flung to them by misguided admirers than they do in assaulting the unwary. Yet it was a swan which used to fly up to Hugh's house at Stow to guard his sleep, take food from his hand, and "bury its head and long neck in his wide sleeves."

Loving and loved, the saints existed. All the ancient stories imply an endearing give and take between them and the creatures they befriended. When James of Cerqueto preached in the open air it was noticed that "the very frogs ceased their croaking at his bidding, to allow his words to be heard." And the tale runs that Brother Benno, a German monk, disturbed in the midst of his meditations while crossing a marsh by equally vociferous frogs, bade them "be Seraphians, since the frogs in Seraphus are mute." The frogs obediently fell silent. But after he had gone a little farther on his way Benno began to repent his crossness, calling to mind the quotation from Daniel, "O ye whales and all that move in the waters, bless ye the Lord." Was it not possible, he argued with himself, that "the singing of the frogs might perchance be more agreeable to God than his own praying?" So he told the frogs that they should "praise God in their accustomed fashion; and soon the air and the fields were vehement with their conversation."

Beasts had their duties, too, the saints felt with very good sense, and should be useful when they could. John Massias of Lima trained a donkey to be a beggar for the needy just as he was himself. The good little creature learned at which houses to expect charity and used to go about alone and gather into its baskets whatever food or clothing the gentlemen of Peru had on hand that day for John's "beloved poor." Columba had his white horse, renowned beast of burden for Iona's monastery, which wept, it is said, when Columba tottered down the path to put on its harness for the last time.

Ignatius Loyola also kept a horse to trot on errands for the Jesuit Hospital at Azpeitia. Spaniards have never been celebrated as animal-lovers, but Ignatius, in spite of the thousand cares that nagged at him while he watched over his fledgling Order, was still inquiring for his "useful little beast" sixteen years after he had left Azpeitia. Happily all was well, for in a charming letter preserved by the Jesuits one hears a certain Father Ochoa assuring him that "the pony is very fast and very good . . . He is a privileged animal in Azpeitia and even when he breaks into cornfields people wink at it."

Then there were saints like Ciaran of Ireland, who put the very inhabitants of the wilderness to work in a good cause—he persuaded deer to pull logs for him when he was building a church beside his hut in the forest. Helenus of Egypt used a crocodile for a ferryboat in time of flood when no one else could cross a swollen river to get to Sunday service. And when Felix of Nola was escaping from persecutors of Christians he "crept through a hole in a ruinous wall which was instantly closed up by spiders' webs." I rejoice that spiders were generous to Felix, he was such a generous fellow himself. If he had two coats, he always gave the better one to the poor; if he had only one he could be counted on to exchange that for the rags of the first beggar he met on the way.

The strangest assistants to any saints were the three companions of Colman of Galway, friend and correspondent to Columba. He lived alone and, although not on Innisfree, in the sort of house all hermits those days built, quite literally "of clay and wattles made." And in it he had room for a cock, a fly, and a mouse, which he fed and spoke to kindly, and all three of which became his servitors. The cock's duty was to crow at the proper hours for matins, a sort of primitive alarm clock. The mouse nibbled his ear when he fell asleep over his studies. And the fly, it was said, kept his place in his books when for some purpose he had to leave them. But as the seasons passed the friends died and Colman mourned for them. In fact he wrote his grief to Columba, who returned him a saint's answer: "Colman, dear fellow, see what happens when people become rich. They cannot bear to lose their riches." And Colman, the tale continues, lived thereafter as a poor hermit should.

Oddly enough, dogs are not so common in the stories as might be expected. Perhaps biographers see nothing strange in the good offices of man's natural friend. Still, there is the faithful Grigio, the huge gray hulking mongrel who made himself bodyguard for Don John Bosco when that energetic and eccentric defender of delinquent boys was trying to found the Salesian Order. Where Grigio came from no one seemed to know any more than they knew the pedigrees of all the hundreds and thousands of homeless children Don John gathered about him. He simply turned up one day when John needed him and fought off a footpad who evidently did not realize how poor the saint kept himself for the sake of his boys. From then on he was continually at hand when John was in danger, which was often. He intercepted foes, warned him once of an ambush, and generally served him better than the Italian police. And when Don John had persuaded Garibaldi's government that he could be trusted to run his schools for waifs, when his projects were thriving and the Order safe, Grigio came once more about dinner time in the refectory. He rubbed his head against John's habit, lifted up a tentative paw, then wandered out into the night and was never seen again. This is no folk tale but a fact—unlike, perhaps, the dog which miraculously fed Saint Rock when that charitable man, having contracted the plague from those he had been nursing, dragged himself into the countryside so that he need not be a burden on the overcrowded hospitals. It was a genuine dog, too, which led John of the Cross out of the courtyard of the monastery where he had been imprisoned and beaten. (The monks there had what seemed to them very good reason for locking John up. He had been trying to reform them.)

Factual or embroidered, all the stories linger like music in the mind, chants of the living charity that can exist and has existed between man and his voiceless brothers. It is perfectly true that Philip Neri used to say mass with a chipmunk perched on his shoulder. And if it is not perfectly true, it is rather charming to read that Petroc, a sixth-century abbot, took a splinter out of the eye of a dragon which came to him for help; or that Cuthbert was generous to ministering eagles. For when he and his acolyte were once on the road and hungry, they prayed for food and the bird caught them a large salmon from the River Teviot. The boy brought it triumphantly to the saint, who at once asked him, "Why did you not give our fisherman a part of it to eat since he, too, was fasting?" And Cuthbert cut the fish in two and returned half to the eagle.

We may believe only half the chronicles, but the very metaphors have a merciful point. And when one stops to think of it, are even the most picturesque of them so miraculous? Old friars and hermits lived very quiet lives. They must have learned to move softly in their wildernesses. So it is not strange that hares or deer or fieldmice —that even bears and foxes—became their companions. In our day a lady in Kenya has taught a lioness to retrieve like a dog and to sleep patiently beside her head. I recently read the confessions of an arctic explorer's wife who found tamed wolves as altruistic a race as she had ever encountered. Then what is so marvelous about Finbarr? He merely milked a doe when cow's milk was in short supply. I find it easy to believe that Theon of Thebaud walked in the desert at night with "the wild things of the desert walking by his side." Love is a worker of more miracles than the ingenuity of a storyteller can invent.

If in our age there are saints living and working among us—and I have no doubt there are—they will be living and working much like their old exemplars. They will be poor, for they must spend all they have on derelicts and needy neighbors. They will be busier than any businessman—rescuing slum dwellers, saving lives in jungle hospitals, teaching trades to Bolivian Indians, helping the migrant workers in California orchards. But when they are at home, wherever home may be (a shed, a tenement, a tent, an Andean hut) they will be sharing quarters with some beast that needs tending. They will be feeding hungry kittens or splinting the leg of an injured seagull or—who knows?—teaching catechism to some garrulous dolphin. For while the old needs remain there will always be some good man to ease them. The patterns of compassion do not change.

The Good Companions

As a saint-watcher, amateur standing, I am forever discovering my own ignorance.

"Saints have this or that quality," I assure myself complacently. Then out of some historical thicket bursts a new specimen, or I come across a whole flock of the brilliant creatures, behaving quite otherwise than I had expected. For the glass through which I observe them may be imperfect but at least it is not *stained* glass. It does not filter out their humanity but lets it shine through unimpaired.

For instance, I used to consider them a bit deficient in the matter of ordinary mortal affection. Not that they did not love their fellow man—no saint could dislike the nation of men and still earn his halo—but the necessity to be loved in return, the relying on the capacities of another for consolation—those were attributes in which I once believed them lacking. Yet the longer I watched, the oftener I found them nearly as busy being attached to some person or troop of persons as the weakest of the rest of us. Not that the affection often got in the way of their progress as it is apt to do in ours. They did their best to discipline their love, to keep it from interfering with their headlong rush toward holiness.

A Benedict whose sister, Scholastica, he calls his "twin soul" meets with her only once a year after each has founded a monastic community. An Ignatius, devoted to Francis Xavier as to no other of his company, sends him off to the ends of the earth, perfectly aware they will not delight again in one another's conversation this side of heaven. A Francis de Sales has his last session with Jane Chantal (and both know it is the last), withholding from her any sort of valedictory emotion. Yet the emotion is visible to the appreciative eye.

As you see, I have deliberately mixed the genders in giving examples of saintly friendships. For, contrary to the sour view taken by saint-loathers, the affection of my favorite heroes and heroines as often as not wreathes itself around someone of the opposite sex. No doubt about it, there are masculine and feminine principles native to the race, and even among the saints one principle complements the other when there is work to be accomplished or simple human needs to be reckoned with. As Frédéric Ozanam has remarked in another connection, "It appears that nothing great can be done in the Church without a woman having a share in it." I would go further. I would say that some of the greatest saints of both sexes seem to soar higher and more daringly feather to feather with the man or the woman who accompanies the flight.

The old hermits may have retired to their huts or their caves and abjured the whole world. But as if to confound their peculiar—and to us inhuman—way of living they had Jerome nearby both to confuse and refute them. He had his Saint Paula, trailing after him wherever he took himself, the one friend able both to love and to calm that truculent scholar. When he left Rome for the desert, so did she, to establish her own community, but to remain in such constant touch with him that he could neither translate the Bible nor govern his monastery without her soothing influence. Even her family was dear to him, including her granddaughter.

There is a letter of his to Paula in which he begs her to let him have the child to educate. "If you send her to me, I shall become her tutor and her nurse," says the

Scourge of the Desert. "I shall carry her on my shoulders, old man though I am, and hold lisping intercourse with her, prouder of my office than ever Aristotle was of his." Since Aristotle's pupil was, of course, Alexander the Great, one may feel the saint is exaggerating as usual. But there is no denying that he gave his harsh old heart to all that was Paula's. When she died he wrote to Theophilus, "The death of Paula has so completely prostrated me that until today I have translated nothing. At one blow I lost all comfort." And he goes on to say that when he tried to write something commemorative about her "the stylus fell from my fingers."

Jerome made more fuss about his loss than seems altogether proper to his professed vocation. But when in 404 the great John Chrysostom fell into disfavor with the Empress Eudoxia—for having told her a few home truths —and had to go into banishment, Saint Olympias grieved so that "it was necessary to tear her from his feet by violence." It is pleasant to hear that John comforted and "encouraged her from his places of exile by letters."

Such excesses of demonstration belong to either a more dramatic age or more dramatic biographers than we are accustomed to. Yet as late as the thirteenth century one finds Saint Edmund of Abingdon, no less a personage than the Archbishop of Canterbury, telling a certain lady whom he had befriended and who had come to pass Holy Week at the cathedral, "You are indeed welcome. And, if the world's judgments were not too harsh for the purity of our intentions, nothing should be allowed ever to part us from each other." Courtly jargon or honest sentiment, it rings happily on the ear.

More in the saintly pattern and also far more romantic is the famous friendship of Clare and Francis of Assisi. It is not easy to follow them accurately, since hagiographers of the period have so hung them with pious stories that they nearly smother under wreaths of artificial flowers. It is unlikely, for example, that Clare any more than Francis was God-haunted from youth. She belonged to a family important and imposing in Assisi, an arrogant household of lords and knights. (Francis came much lower in the social scale, since his father was a merchant even though an affluent one.) No doubt, since she is supposed to have been very pretty, she was as full of small prides and vanities as any other girl of her age and station. All we really know about her before she put on the Franciscan habit and founded the Poor Clares is that she had suitors whom she refused; that when her family grew annoyed at her obstinacy in not choosing one whom they particularly favored she went to her aunt, a certain Sister Bona, for comfort; and that Sister Bona, probably as a special treat, took her to hear the odd Little Poor Man preach. One suspects it was the substitute in those days to taking her to a matinee or for a day's shopping in town. After all, Francis's dramatic conversion and his eccentricities were prime gossip in Assisi just then.

Bona, however, did more than merely entertain Clare with the town's sensation. She also took her, as it were, backstage—to meet the friar himself at the Portiuncula, where his group lived in such lively and joyous poverty. Clare was eighteen at the time and probably longing for something remarkable to happen to her. What happened, of course, was Francis.

Whether she caught fire at the beginning—whether it was spiritual love at first sight—we have no way of knowing. The only thing biographers truly agree on is that the meetings, chaperoned by Bona but always clandestine (for to her grand relatives Francis must have seemed no better than a mad and mendicant clown) went on for about a year; and at some time during the year Clare decided the vocation of Francis must be her own. Then came the celebrated Elopement. Late at night on Palm Sunday Clare let herself out of her house by the little "door of death"— the side door which in many homes was opened only to carry out the dead—and headed for the Portiuncula. She had dressed herself like a bride complete to veil and all her jewels, a romantic Italianate touch both saints had evidently planned in advance as a symbolic flourish. Francis met her at the chapel, took off the bridal clothes, cut her hair, and dressed her in the same sort of rough, undyed cloak he himself wore.

Since she patently could not stay on with the friars, she went first to a Benedictine convent nearby and eventually to another refuge, and was at last able to found her own order, which maintained as nearly as was possible to women of that day the same rule of total poverty Francis had insisted on for his own community. (Many of the earlier stories say that Clare's family rode out angrily to drag her back from sanctuary, and it is certainly possible they strenuously objected to her runaway adventure. But since her mother and two of her sisters eventually joined her community, it certainly looks as if the objections did not last as long or were not as aggressive as the tales contend.) In any event she found her final haven at San Damiano, not far from Francis's house, and Clare was never to leave it again except to visit the Portiuncula from time to time; and even that pleasure was at length denied her by a puritanical Pope who could not understand the remarkable relationship between the two shining saints.

Unworldly innocents! Clare had imagined herself wandering about the country, free as Francis to do good deeds and speak ecstatic words. Such an ideal in the twelfth century was about as capable of coming true as was Francis's dream of converting the Sultan in one interview. So she stayed enclosed like other nuns of her era. But the two friends were faithful to the end—"Do not believe," said Francis, "that I do not love her with a perfect love"— and between them they invigorated not only Italy but Christian Europe. They kindled, as Remy de Gourmont has said, "a new poetry, a new art, a renewed religion."

The seventeenth century, if less romantic, took a more tolerant view of woman's role in society. So when along came a saint like Vincent de Paul he was able to lean without scandal on his magnificent Louise de Marillac as

steadfastly as Florence Nightingale depended on her un-
derpraised, overworked Sidney Herbert. Louise and M.
Vincent, as the world has learned lovingly to nickname him,
not only prodded France out of its lethargic attitude toward the poor but established orders and organizations
for social justice which have lasted to this day.

Vincent by himself was a tornado of compassionate energy. He was God's wrathful man, outraged that so many
of his countrymen had nothing while the rich lived plac-
idly in luxury. No condition was too wretched for him not
to try to relieve. Without Louise, however, there was
many a distressed case he could not properly handle. He
had enlisted the aristocratic women of Paris into a league
called the Ladies of Charity, which is still very much in
existence. And they, fired by his anger and his plead-
ing, poured out their alms as well as their time to help
him. But it is easy to see why he could use a different
sort of assistant. The Ladies were kind, they were generous;
but they were dilettantes. Money, gracious gestures, fine
sewing—those they could provide. But who was to go
into the hovels and the hospitals to deal with rough
actualities of baby-tending and physical nursing? Nobody,
really, except Louise (his right hand as well as part of his
great heart) and the peasants and country women whom
both saints recruited, quite aware that the high-born had
no monopoly on charity.

These peasant women might need overseeing and instruction, since many of them were as illiterate as they
were well intentioned. And there beside him was Louise,
panting to serve both as tutor and leader. Neither saint
seems to have had any idea of founding a new religious
order. What is now the famous Sisters of Charity grew
up rather by itself, as such comradeships tend to do. The
harder they worked, the more dedicated became Louise's
little band, until they demanded that they be allowed to
take vows—rather as volunteer soldiers for a local war
decide they need the discipline of a regiment and a leader.
But Vincent was adamant about any such nonsense as an

enclosed group. He wanted no collection of nuns who shut themselves away from a world he meant to change. "Your convent," he told them, "will be the house of the sick; your cell, a hired room; your cloister, the streets of the city or the wards of the hospital."

Nor did they fail him any more than did Louise. Indeed, so close in spirit were this zealous man and this fiery woman that they were like the twin souls of Benedict and Scholastica. Again, theirs is an example of the masculine and feminine principles harnessing themselves together for the relief of the world's misery and the glory of God.

One would have been less without the other. Over and over, history contradicts the popular notion that saints must walk singly toward virtue, lonely as the Phoenix. Augustine has his Melania; Bernard, his Duchess of Lorraine. Martin de Porres depended on Rose of Lima (or perhaps she on him) and what an odd friendship *that* must have been, between half-caste Martin, gentlest of holy men, and the extravagantly ascetic Rose. Philip Neri and his Catherine of Ricci never met, but their letters flew back and forth like homing pigeons.

Alphonsus de Ligouri (the same Alphonsus who in his salad days went to the opera without his spectacles so he could hear the music without seeing the half-draped chorus) has his gifted if opinionated Marie Celeste. Reading about the trouble she caused him, one has a suspicion that she must have been as much his hairshirt as his friend; but with her visions and her determination to reform the Order of the Visitandines over the protests of the community and the diocese, she found in Alphonsus exactly the right man. He had been a lawyer before he became a religious and he had all a lawyer's love for a fine-spun argument. The stories allege that as an attorney he never in fifteen years lost a case, although that embellishment seems to me nearly as legendary as some of the voyages of Brendan, the Irish sailor monk. What *is* true is the fact that Alphonsus gave up the law in one passionate moment because he found he had won a case only by an error of his own in reading his brief. At any rate, he had not forgotten his training, and he burrowed into her allegations as carefully as if they formed part of a secular lawsuit; and he persuaded both himself and the papal authorities that the Visitandines should indeed be reformed along the lines her mystical voices had recommended. If only Joan of Arc had known an Alphonsus, perhaps the stake might have lost a victim and the playwrights a heroine nearly as useful to them as Cinderella.

Those were sober days in which Marie and Alphonsus lived. There seems to be nothing playful or amusing about their affection for one another. In the Dark Ages, however, the times may have been wilder but demonstrations of sentiment were more acceptable. Boniface, for instance, made no bones about his love for smiling Lioba, whom he called his "dear one." Men and women of his era believed firmly in displays of emotion even between men and women who were saints.

Christopher Dawson terms Boniface a "shockingly neglected" figure, a Christian humanist living twelve hundred years ago who "had a deeper influence on the history of Europe than any Englishman who ever lived." He was an apostle, a teacher, and a Benedictine missioner from his island to the tribes beyond the Rhine who had only lately and half-heartedly adopted Christianity. His task was enormous, since he needed not only to civilize and educate the people but to tame their savage kings. Nor could he have done it so successfully if he had not had Lioba and her little group of nuns to help him. The adventure he summoned them to was a great novelty. Ladies in those days who had taken the veil lived enclosed in their safe, often luxurious convents; it was a dangerous world beyond those abbey walls. Yet when Boniface sent for Lioba to bring her own civilizing influence to the barbarous Franks, she went as willingly as if he had invited her to a luncheon party. And from his letters, many of which still exist, we know how much he loved and valued her. The most touching of them asks that she consent to be buried with him in the same grave, "so that their bodies might await the day of resurrection together." Even Paula and Jerome could scarcely match that for tenderness.

There is one couple, however, who in an entertaining way carried on a friendship so worldly that if one does not take into account the flowery language of the sixth century (particularly when the language was often Latin) it might lift a few eyebrows. The friends were Radegund, the Abbess of Poitiers, and Venantius Fortunatus, Bishop of the same diocese. Radegund is written down in Butler as a woman very penitential and holy. But Fortunatus, like some other saints of the period who got elevated to the calendar by local acclaim, seems less to wear a halo than the equivalent of a top hat. His only claim to sanctity that I can uncover is the fact that he was a poet who wrote a great many graceful Latin verses and such famous hymns as *"Vexilla Regis"* and the *"Salve Festa Dies,"* the latter still sometimes sung at Easter.

Radegund may have mortified herself, fasted, and prayed in quite the approved fashion of that day, but from the tone of Fortunatus's letters to her, she certainly limited her austerities to personal ones and indulged her pet bard like the "mother" he persisted in calling her. The correspondence, if frivolous by some standards, is charming. They send each other gifts. He writes verses to her, thanks her for feasts she has given him, enumerating the various dishes such as meat served on a silver plate, vegetables on a marble dish "tasting sweet as the honey which flavored them," fruit, cream, chestnuts, pastries. In fact, the man seems as devoted to the table as he was to delicate and festive poetry. Perhaps he reformed later and died as holy a soul as Butler himself could wish. But when he is dispatching those letters to the abbess, he sounds a very relaxed and vivacious sort of saint. And so, in spite of her fame for good works, does she. (Fortunatus refers to her "delicious and versatile humor" and once to a game of chance they played together in the abbey parlor.) Or she may simply have been a lesser Teresa, believing that virtue took no harm when it went hand in hand with merriment.

And that they were fond of one another there is no doubt at all. He once wrote her a Latin verse during Lent, begging that she not shut herself up so closely just because it *is* Lent, and saying winningly, "Even though the clouds have gone and the sky is serene, the day is sunless when you are absent." What a man for a phrase! And how the dovecote must have fluttered when Fortunatus came visiting.

Personally, I have a sneaking fondness for him even though he may have rattled to heaven merely on the strength of his ability to beguile the abbey or to break into verse on every suitable occasion. And it is to the honor of both him and Radegund that they humanized their diocese. Both loved learning, loved civilized living, and, in their own manner, probably loved God quite a lot, too.

It is a far and perilous flight from this sixth-century pair to the friendship between Teresa and Saint John of the Cross, her diminutive but mighty "half a monk." One might as well compare wrens and skylarks. These poets, mystics, Doctors of the Church, belong to a totally different order of beings. Probably no such pair in the annals of Christendom have so ravished the hearts and intellects of believing —even unbelieving—mankind. Yet they, too, were good companions in both the worldly and the supernatural sense. One amplified the other; they supported one another while they reformed the Carmelite Order, and found in their opposing temperaments the refreshment they required. Each might have been a lesser person if they had not come together at the right moment in history.

So, too, one supposes, would have been the delightful pair (and my last entry for these particular stakes) whom I mentioned at the beginning of the chapter. They were Jane Chantal and Francis de Sales, beloved in their own day and still enchanting in ours. Their friendship was a quieter one than Teresa's and John's, less romantic than that of the Assisian duo. But it was equally steadfast. It is also easy to spy on, since we have the letters de Sales wrote to Jane in the marvelous style which is still the pride of France. Unfortunately, and absurdly one feels, at his death Jane burnt the letters she had written to him and which he had carefully numbered and annotated. But at least we have his half of the correspondence and can understand from it the tenderness, the respect, and the real love he felt for this headstrong but intelligent young widow of whom he once said, "In Madame Chantal I have found the valiant woman whom Solomon had difficulty finding in Jerusalem."

The letters are naturally much concerned with spiritual matters, for Jane was very conscious of her soul, and Francis was a celebrated counselor. But they also abound in personal references, in sunny asides, in little quips and teasings. "I have to laugh," begins many a sentence, and the joke is usually on himself. Or he thanks her for a "length of cloth" she has sent him. "Never will a garment have kept me so warm as this; for its warmth will go straight to my heart, and I shall not think it is purple, but rather crimson and scarlet." (Of course he plans to give it to the poor, but he is too soft-hearted to tell her that.)

During the last eight years of their friendship, they saw each other seldom—Jane being busy with the duties of the order she had founded and Francis obsessed with the cares of his turbulent territory where he was attempting (with success) to win back the country from the Calvinists. And at the last meeting, as I have said, he refused to give her any guidance at all. Her education at his hands, he must have felt, was complete, their work together done. She had dozens of questions to ask him, but instead of answering her Francis hesitated. "Wait," he told her. "Listen for a minute."

What he wanted her to hear was his servant, Charles, whistling some graceful tune outside the door. It was as if he were saying, "Don't be so self-conscious, my dear. Learn how to enjoy the casual, unexpected pleasures of God's world."

I could name a hundred other examples of sustaining affection between saints but they would only encumber the point I wish to make—that love of virtue does not restrict human love. The heart is an organ that can expand to hold the world. The more love it contains, the greater its capacity for containing extra supplies.

And as I mentioned at first, there is something especially fetching about the comradeship between men and women geniuses. Ours is a carnal time, with every relationship suspect or explained away by psychiatry. It restores the spirit to learn that there can be friendships where nothing is asked and everything given; where innocence flourishes as if there had never been a Fall.

A Cell of One's Own

History must always be taken with a grain of salt. It is, after all, not a science but an art, as the Greeks knew; so that when they were parceling out the deities, they gave history a Muse of her own just as they assigned one each to poetry and playwriting and music and other explosions of the imagination.

I was reminded of this truth only yesterday morning. I had picked up for an hour's refreshment that exquisite but perverse essay of Virginia Woolf's, "A Room of One's Own." One bleak sentence caught my skeptical eye. "Nothing," it said flatly, "is known about women before the eighteenth century."

Now Mrs. Woolf the novelist is a delight. Mrs. Woolf the historian is something else again. If I put my trust in her I must believe that until recently women had been a voiceless, hopeless multitude, without power or influence in the world. I must take for granted the odd idea that we moderns who write and paint and manage corporations and elect Presidents sprang full-panoplied from the forehead of the Nineteenth Amendment. I am perfectly willing to grant my sex an astonishing adaptability, but I cannot give such a theory as Mrs. Woolf's a full assent.

Naturally I'm grateful for the ballot and my Rights just as I'm grateful for automatic dish-washers, air-conditioning, penicillin, and other latter-day luxuries. But I doubt that, even unenfranchised, our ancestresses were so underprivileged a group as feminist history makes them out. They did not lash themselves to railings in their drive toward equality with men, or go on hunger strikes. But in that they admitted no impediment to their abilities, they were, in a way, the first feminists. And anyone who contends that there were no great women before the eighteenth century has not read history with any care.

What about Bridget of Sweden, born in 1303, who made peace treaties as other women now run up slip covers? Or Lioba, who brought learning, gentleness, and the arts to heathen Germans in the seventh century? Or Joan of Arc, burned not for her sex but her politics? What, in short, about the saints?

For from the beginning of the Christian era women, no matter what their position in society, knew another outlet for their talents beside the purely domestic. They had only to step from the hearth to the cloister and find there a bracing freedom. If we wish to catch a glimpse of the New Woman as typified in a different age, we need look no farther than the female saints. From old abbesses of desert monasteries to the nineteenth century's Mother Javouhey —whom Louis-Philippe of France called "that great man"— there they stand, articulate, vigorous, and unsubduable. Some of them were queens; some of them were peasants. They lived in times of storm or of calm. They were as well educated as Hilda or as illiterate as Catherine of Siena. But not one of them seems to have found her sex a barrier to greatness. I could count them by hundreds if I had need, valiant women all and powers in their generations. But five does as well as fifty. The five I mean to mention come from different ages and from varying nations. They have in common only their genius and the fact that they star the saintly Calendar.

I suppose, of the list, Teresa of Avila seems nearest to us. Although she lived in fanatic Spain more than four hundred years ago, her unconquerable charm works on us today just as it did on the kings, townspeople, and recalcitrant nuns of her own time. She was that near contradiction, a reformer with a sense of humor.

"God deliver us from sullen saints!" she used to cry, and there was never one less long-faced than she. Only a genius could have spoken with such familiarity to God— "No wonder You have so few friends when You treat the ones You have so badly"—and sounded not like a scold but a lover.

Teresa's story runs counter to that of many men and women who worked great changes on society. Her vocation seems unapparent in her youth. As a girl in the province of old Castile, she was pretty, clever, romantic, and lively, but no more than that. It is true that at seven she and her brother, Rodrigo, decided to run away to find martyrdom among the Moors in Africa. Carrying a stock of dried raisins (Teresa was always practical), they got as far as the open country outside Avila's walls before they were met by their Uncle Francisco and brought back home. But such an escapade was rather like a modern child's running away to join a circus, a common romantic dream. Otherwise Teresa lived the ordinary life of a Spanish young lady of good family. She read novels, attended balls, and took pains with her dress. We know that she was attractive and aware of the fact. At a party a few days before she entered the Carmelite Convent, a young man was admiring her pretty feet in their dancing slippers. "Take a good look, sir," Teresa told him. "You won't be getting another chance."

It was only at past twenty when she decided after much heart-searching to become a nun that she caught fire— became, indeed, a conflagration which burned up the corruption of her day. For that religion was corrupt then does not stand in doubt. The Inquisition had terrorized but not cleansed Spain. The convent where Teresa went as a novice and eventually presided as its prioress had once been strict, poor, and holy. Now it was like half the other establishments of its kind, a twittering bird cage of femininity with its rules relaxed and its practices tarnished. Girls came there not for love of God but to "find a home," and they continued to be as worldly as if they still lived in society. They gave concerts and parties, wore jewelry, dined on delicacies sent by their families, and entertained friends in the parlors. It was Teresa's lifelong task to recover the ancient Rule of the Carmelites and to bring not only her foundation but the whole of Spain back to pure practices of religion.

That she did not do it without outcry, controversy, and discouragement goes without saying. She was as beleaguered and reviled as any suffragette of the nineteenth century agitating for the vote. Nuns and priests who did not wish to change their soft ways of living demonstrated violently against her. Avila for a while ostracized her. She was examined by the Inquisition. An irate Papal Nuncio called her a "restless gadabout" and cried, "She is ambitious and teaches theology as though she were a Doctor of the Church." (The joke after some centuries is on him, for Teresa *is* now regarded, if unofficially, as a Doctor of the Church.) She seems, however, to have been as little afraid of nuncios as she was of princes, prioresses, or the surly muleteers who carried her on her interminable journeys.

Merry and undaunted, she "traipsed" as she says, about Spain, re-establishing the Unmitigated Rule in convent after convent, reforming, exhorting, and captivating the countryside.

With her eloquence and charm she won over the Archbishop of Seville, who instead of permitting her to kneel to him fell on his own knees in front of her. She successfully lectured the Pope. Even the formidable King Philip found his letters from her studded with good advice. She traveled continually, enduring floods, cold, heat, lack of provisions, and unspeakable country inns with the hardihood of an old soldier. "God gives us much to suffer for Him," she wrote, "if only from fleas, ghosts, and bad roads."

Yet, for all her traveling, she found time to write the great books, *The Way of Perfection* and *The Interior Cas-*

tle, on which rest her literary fame, as well as to take a lively interest in her horde of friends, to look out for the welfare of her beloved family, and to bring up various little nieces sent her from time to time in the casual Spanish fashion. For Teresa, besides being an inspired executive and a holy woman, was also an enchanting companion. She believed that joy was quite as essential to sanctity as faith or good works. She used to leave her prayers in order to visit with her community when they begged for her company. She set the nuns dancing to castanets on feast days and encouraged laughter and music as heartily as she discouraged sullen faces and sin. That what she did was done for love of God rather than for human satisfaction does not blur her charm even for the agnostic. In fact, anyone who writes about Teresa finds himself falling in love with his subject. Here is Woman as Reformer at her merry best—talented, original, unself-conscious, and powerful, filled like other geniuses with the "large drafts of intellectual day" which Crashaw ascribes to her.

Because Teresa was herself a writer we come close to her. We can look at another famous woman, Hilda of Whitby, only through the eyes of her biographer, the Venerable Bede. That busy little English monk wrote history with a pen dipped in incense. All his stories are nosegays, sweet-smelling as pinks or freesias. But Hilda, even engarlanded, comes through with her capabilities intact. She was no journeyer like Teresa, but then her country, in the early seventh century, was no place for journeys; it was barely scratched by civilization. The Romans had gone, leaving their walls and their roads and their villas to crumble away in the forests. The Saxons had only recently conquered the Druid Celts, who worshiped oak trees and burned human sacrifices alive. It seems almost unthinkable that such a great woman could have risen to acclaim in so savage a land. Yet when we meet Hilda in her thirties, she is already abbess of the great double monastery at Streaneschalah (afterward re-named Whitby by the Danes) and in charge of both the monks and the nuns there. To be

sure, this coeducational kind of establishment was not rare
is those days. Evidently women were more highly considered in rough-and-tumble times than we believe. Although the two communities lived apart, coming together
only to sing their Office in choir, many a group of monks
obeyed an abbess rather than an abbot.

Perhaps men then were like their counterparts today,
inclined to leave teaching and the small arts to women
while they went about their business of making a living or
waging war or bringing home the venison for the pot, so
that abbesses were more likely to know Latin and Greek
than their brothers. Or it might simply have been that
women proved the better dormitory mistresses, less jealous
of authority and better equipped to see to creature comforts. At any rate, Hilda was one of those abbesses, and a
famous one. She was famous for her learning; she was
renowned for her charity. She was celebrated as an educator and statesman. And this in the darkest period of what
we call the Dark Ages, when, we are told, a woman knew
little more than how to keep a fire burning under the kettle
or the best way of mending her husband's tunic. It shows
how histories disagree.

Hilda insisted on study. All her community read the
Scriptures, and copied and pored over what books they
could acquire in that long-ago time nearly eight hundred
years before the invention of the printing press. They illuminated manuscripts. They worked at involved mathe-
matical riddles. She herself, in addition to scholarship, la-
bored at looking after the welfare of all who lived in the
territory governed by her monastery. Bede writes that "not
only ordinary people but even kings and princes asked
and accepted her advice."

So highly was she regarded that when the Great Synod
of 664 was called to decide on certain Church doctrine,
Whitby was chosen on account of its reputation for learning. One wonders if Hilda's equal reputation for hospitality
might not have also influenced the committees. Although

she ate sparingly herself, she "kept a dainty table," and bishops are seldom averse to a tasty dinner.

But if Hilda had done nothing else worth reporting we could still love her for one famous deed. She came close to inventing English literature.

There lived in her abbey, as a servant, a man named Caedmon, who according to Bede had never been able to sing or to play the harp until in a dream someone called him by name, saying "Caedmon, sing to me."

"What shall I sing?" he asked.

"Sing me of Creation," came the answer, and Caedmon at once began "to sing in praise of God."

The dreamer mentioned his new gift to the alderman of the town; the alderman told Hilda. And Hilda at once took him under her motherly wing.

"Then the Abbess began to accept and to love the gift of God to this man and she advised him that he leave the world and receive monkhood; and he consented to that gladly. And," continues Bede, "his song and his poetry were so winsome that his teachers wrought and learned at his mouth."

It may be that Hilda personifies all women everywhere who have been accused of inheriting no genius comparable to man's. Perhaps like her they have been kept so occupied persuading men to sing or to paint or to explore the stars, that they have had little time to conquer the arts themselves. Certainly literature would have been poorer without Hilda's patronage of the first native English poet.

Hilda is only the most eminent of dozens of great abbesses who ruled and dispensed justice and kept learning alight during those dark old times. Elburga, Radegund, Agnes, Hildegard, Mildred—one could count them off like a litany. There was Lioba, already mentioned, who thought nothing of following her cousin, Saint Boniface, into the astonishing wilderness of Germany to convert the pagans there, and to whom all of Hesse and Saxony came "in peril of fire and tempest and sickness." There was Caesaria, who fourteen hundred years ago drew up a course of study for her community and saw to it that they "studied two hours of every day." There was Walburga, who practiced skillfully such medicine as existed in the eighth century and suffered after death an unusual fate. She was one of the band of brave women who accompanied Lioba on her travels, and she became as renowned on the Continent as in her native England. But her name took on a sea change in the northern countries, where the most common version of it is Walpurgis. It was on her feast day, evidently, that wild revels of Walpurgis Night took place, a queer tribute to this kindly saint.

Saint Audrey, the abbess of Ely, suffered an even quainter metamorphosis. She reigned over a populous community in the seventh century and must have been one of the most beloved of Anglo-Saxon holy people, since so many old churches in England are named for her. Whatever else she did, she added an adjective to the language. Her feast, like Walburga's, was kept with such enthusiasm for many years that, like other holy days which turn into a time for secular romping, June 23 became famous for its annual fairs. The fairs drew customers and the customers wanted things to buy; so cheap necklaces and other trumperies were always on sale, and eventually the name "Saint Audrey" was corrupted into "tawdry." It seems a poor memento for a useful life.

But not all feminine saints were prioresses. Margaret of Scotland entered no convent and took no vows. She was a mother, a wife, and a queen who ran her realm, Scotland, like the talented headmistress of a turbulent boarding school. "Margaret," says one biographer, "had queenship thrust upon her." When she was a girl of not much more than twelve, in 1057, she was sent to the English court of Edward the Confessor to be reared and educated. After Edward died and the Normans reigned in England, Margaret took refuge in Scotland with Malcolm Canmore, called "the Great Leader." Margaret was "as good as she was beautiful," and Malcolm fell in love with her. He was an exemplary soldier but not much of a courtier or a

scholar, and it took his pretty Queen some years to tame
him. As a matter of fact, although she taught him to leave
off his rougher ways, to go to church, to "be attentive to
the works of justice, mercy, almsgiving, and other virtues,"
he seems never to have learned to read. But "he would
turn over and examine books which the Queen used either
for her devotions or her study; and whenever he heard
her express especial liking for a particular book, he also
would look at it with special interest, kissing it and often
taking it into his hands." What an appreciative husband he
appears to have been!

Indeed, there in the eleventh century, he seems a prototype of all those husbands whom psychologists rather
scold today. He fought the wars but Margaret did the
ruling. She had a strange, disturbed country for her domain. The clergy kept to their Celtic calendars and observed their Celtic feasts instead of following the Latin
pattern. The people were wild, superstitious, and ignorant.
Highwaymen flourished, common as heather on the
moors, and a traveler went in fear of his life. Margaret
stirred herself to root out as many evils as one woman
could manage in a lifetime. She insisted on education for
both clergy and lay people. She built hostels for strangers,
ransomed captives, founded almshouses and hospitals for
the sick and the poor. She was politician, statesman,
mother-confessor to the land. Like Hilda, she also presided over a great synod which separated the Celtic
Church from its old practices and wrestled it into line with
the rest of Christendom. "It was Margaret's tremendous
achievement," says one authority, "to open her doors to
the full wealth of the Western European tradition, not
by way of conquest and bloodshed but by the joyous generosity that is the gift of the saint."

She was also a pioneer in another sphere. Bands of
women met together at her invitation to study, discuss the
Scriptures, and embroider vestments and altar cloths
for the churches. So we can call Margaret the inventor of
the Women's Club.

She had a further capability, one perhaps rarer even than her other gifts. She was a wise mother. "Her children surpassed in good behavior many who were their elders; they were always affectionate and peaceable among themselves." Across ten centuries I, for one, salute her. No wonder she was able to bequeath to her adopted country "the happiest two hundred years of its history."

But, one might argue, thrones make greatness possible. Besides, Margaret lived during the Middle Ages, before the strictures and anxieties of urbanized civilization had hardened nations and religion into rigid formalism. Contrary to superstition, the society of her time was an open one. Ideas flowed freely from country to country. Christian spoke to infidel with less than anger. Women held both pride and place. By the fourteenth century things had changed enough to corrupt an innocent and universal Christianity and to push many women back into a sort of purdah.

The most shining name of that troubled century, however, is that of Catherine, Siena's saint and still most famous citizen. And she was neither noble nor a scholar. She, at whose bidding princes put down their arms and popes changed their ways of life, was born in 1347, the youngest of the twenty-five children of Giacomo Benincasa, a dyer, and his wife Lapa. Poor Lapa. She has not come off very well at the hands of biographers. They make her out a temper-ridden woman, cross and sharp-tongued. But having to cope with twenty-five lively children as well as a disobedient mystic seems to me excuse enough for a hard word now and then.

Actually, her only faults appear to have been that same quick tongue and the perfectly natural ambition that her yellow-haired Catherine should make a good marriage. She was no visionary but a mother, and she could not for the life of her understand why her daughter should be plagued with extravagant holiness. One fancies her saying to herself, "Adolescents! Forever dramatizing themselves!

We'll see what a bit of discipline will do for those day dreams."

So she nagged the girl to marry until Catherine in a gesture of defiance cut off all her beautiful hair. Any mother might well be annoyed at that, and Lapa did her best to exorcise what she thought of as the devil out of her stubborn child. She set her doing the hardest work of the household, deprived her of her bedroom, and forced her to wait on the rest of the family like a servant. Catherine, however, was a match for her peppery parent. She simply did as she was told so charmingly that in frustration her father and finally her mother gave way in everything. Catherine was allowed to lead her own extraordinary life—to shut herself up to prayer and meditation in a little cell of her own. Almost all saints begin so. They spend an early time of physical inactivity and mystical exercise, like athletes preparing for a contest. Indeed, that is what they are: athletes of the spirit. Catherine was a prodigy, and long before she was twenty her preparations were done and she left her cell to begin a mission to the world.

At first she went into the hospitals and the houses of the poor. A plague swept Italy, and she nursed the sick with the same single-mindedness she had expended on her prayers. The sweetness of her nature and the success of her work so endeared her to Siena that in a year or two she became the center of a group of notable disciples. This fellowship, called the Caterinati, consisted of "old and young, priests and laymen, poets and politicians," most of whom she had rescued from lives of illness, idleness, or vice. One of them was the artist Andrew Vanni, who painted the portrait we still have of her. Another was Neri de Landoccio, the poet. The rest followed a dozen different professions. They were united only as followers of this indomitable girl whom they affectionately called "Mama" although she was younger than any of them.

From Siena her fame spread to all of Italy and eventually to the rest of Europe. She advised kings. She intervened between political war parties. She helped draw up treaties of peace. At this time the Pope was living in exile in Avignon, and Rome had nearly fallen apart for lack of central government. Catherine performed the tremendous feat of coaxing a timorous pontiff back to his proper see in the face of hostility and the arguments of France, which preferred that the Pope live in its sphere of influence. Although Catherine never learned to write, she did learn to dictate, and her letters, addressed to half the great of Europe, are famous for their persuasive skill and boldness of insight. She also composed two books, *The Dialogues of Catherine* and *A Treatise of Divine Providence*, which theologians for years discussed and pondered.

She died at thirty-three, so renowned that she has been called "the greatest woman in Christendom." The whole world wept for her. Her character was so original and inflexible that she does not come through to us so delightfully as does, say, Teresa. But her political and moral triumphs were as enormous as her personal prestige. The historian who belittles feminine talent before the eighteenth century is unwise to overlook her.

Catherine, although all the civilized earth was affected by her life, scarcely ever left home. Mother Javouhey, fifth in this gallery of the great, scarcely ever stopped traveling.

Like the Apostle Paul, she found herself "in journeys often," sailing back and forth across oceans, making her way through jungles and forests and fever-teeming swamps, riding when she could, walking when she must, tramping the roads of earth like a saint and a soldier. Indeed, "General Javouhey" was her nickname in France. Her principal work lay among Africans and Indians, among the slaves, colonists, and savage tribes whom France had recently taken under treaty in Martinique, Guadeloupe, Madagascar, Miquelon, Oceania, the Comoro Archipelago, French Guiana, and a dozen lesser islands. Land swarming with tropical snakes and insects, countries full of gold and of adventurers in search of gold, provinces of torren-

tial rains or murderous heat—those were the parishes of
this amazing woman, born Anne Marie Javouhey in 1779,
in prosperous, wine-growing Burgundy.

Her father, Balthazar, was a well-to-do peasant with his
own vines and acres. On the face of it one might think a
Burgundian farm no place to foster a career of adventure,
but Anne Marie, whom everybody affectionately called
"Nanette," grew up in an adventurous time, the time of
Revolution and the Reign of Terror. In many ways France
then was like France under the German Occupation
twenty-five years ago. To be out of sympathy with the
regime was to go in terror of one's life. There were a Re-
sistance Force and an Underground movement, of which
Burgundy was the center. Instead of sheltering British or
American fliers as in the last war, the Javouheys and their
neighbors rescued priests with a price upon their heads
or members of titled families destined for the guillotine.
As a child of twelve or thirteen, Nanette made quite a
name for herself in the countryside, carrying messages,
hiding the hunted under the very noses of the Secret Police, protecting fugitives fleeing to England. No wonder
she was too restless to settle down later to a staid life as
the wife of some substantial farmer or as her father's helper
on the land. Balthazar had hoped for the latter. He called
Nanette his "clever son" and said she was the best farmer
in the family.

But saints' parents seem to have little say in the matter
of their children's career. Nanette, once the Revolution was
over, determined to follow a religious life where she could
continue to help those in need of help. The habit of kindness thrives on practice. Charity is an infection hard to
shake off. Since schools had been disrupted during the long
troubles of France, the girl came to the conclusion that
she could most usefully work among neglected children.
And Balthazar was no Lapa. If his daughter insisted on
feeding the hungry and teaching the illiterate, she should
have her way. With a saintlike patience of his own he not
only let her take vows and carry off her three sisters and a

brother to do the same, but for a while constituted himself the prop and stay of Nanette's new little order of Saint Joseph of Cluny. He gave them a house. He would turn up with a wagonload of food, frequently in the nick of time, when the sisters had nothing left in the cupboard to eat.

After early trials, the order flourished. Mother Anne Marie grew famed as teacher, nurse, worker of wonders among the poor, the ill, and the insane. In the Napoleonic Wars she nursed French and Austrians impartially, an early Florence Nightingale. But oddly enough she had always dreamed of taking care of "black men." Opportunity came along, as it often does for genius. The governor of Bourbon Island had recently arrived in Paris with tales of ignorance, immorality, and squalor among settlers and natives there. Who in France was brave enough to undertake that mission? "I know just the person for you," said the Minister of the Interior. "Mother Javouhey. She hasn't an ounce of fear in her."

So began her years of work and wandering. Her mission started in Bourbon, went on to Senegal, embraced finally the entire African and South American empire of the French state. It would seem a miraculous accomplishment at any time. But remember that this was the early eighteen hundreds, the Jane Austen period of curls, fainting fits, and helpless femininity. The Sisters of Saint Joseph either were a hundred years ahead of their time or had never been told that they should faint and sigh. We have an amusing picture of what they did expect from themselves. When the Prince de Joinville visited their leper settlement in Guiana, he asked one of the sisters what he could give her as a gift. "Something really useful for you, Sister," he insisted. She asked—and got—a fine gun. After that her invalids had fresh game once or twice a week.

Mother Javouhey had many times to wish that "men were as resolute as women" when she was battling alone with her nuns in the jungle against climate, accident, and the incompetence of administrations. Still, it was a good

time for Anne Marie's abilities. The Revolution, horror that
it was, had still left behind one legacy of good—the idea of
freedom for all peoples. Emancipation was in the air. In
spite of political laxness and dark populations who, as
Mother Javouhey complained, "had learned nothing from
the French except their bad habits," France honestly
wished to release its colonies from the wickedness of slavery. How then to coax those backward tribes into fitness
for citizenship? Man after man, governor after governor
had already failed. Mother Javouhey set out to succeed
where they had not.

She was successful in Bourbon and Senegal, even being
asked by the British to take over their hospitals along with
her own. She was successful in Guadeloupe, Martinique,
Saint-Pierre, Pondicherry. She knew how to farm. She
knew how to manage people. She was adept at country
trades. First she set up hospitals and leper colonies; then
she established schools. After that she began to train natives and settlers for the skills they needed to survive in
an agricultural community. Not for nothing had Anne Marie learned to work in the fields with her father. Now she
applied that knowledge to a new world.

"Grow rice for food," she told the colonists. "When you
plant banana trees, place them twelve feet apart in all
directions so that coffee can grow between them." She
stocked the farms with fat cows, sheep, goats, pigs, don-
keys. She built a brickyard so there would be material
for houses and churches and town offices. Nothing was
too large and nothing too small for Mother Javouhey to
take an interest in, so long as it helped her flock.

Eventually she was asked to take on the most difficult
task of all, the colonization of the Mana district in Guiana.
It was a tremendous request. What she was expected to
do was nothing less than to bring civilization to the most
primitive forests of South America. No one had plans to
offer her, only a chart of repeated failures. Anne Marie
invented her own plan and it was masterful. With thirty-
six nuns, a number of French artisans, and fifty Negro

laborers, she set out for Guiana and in four years had there a prosperous settlement. As she civilized, she also extended her deeds of mercy, buying up runaway slaves to save them from the lash, healing the sick, founding villages for lepers—all as part of the day's work. Once the colony was self-sustaining, she sailed home, only to be asked at once to return to Guiana.

The government proposed to free a group of slaves in Mana and to permit them to be citizens. But they must be taught to read and write and work. Would Mother Javouhey undertake this task—invent, as it were, a master chart for liberation everywhere?

She would and she did. Back she sailed to beard the wrath of French planters, who did not at all like being deprived of cheap slave labor. Considering the temper of the times, it is rather as if a woman were to set out to teach hostile Afrikaners how to do away with apartheid. Angry planters even bribed someone to upset a boat with Mother Javouhey in it. She proved unsinkable. What she did do was found a state within a state. She selected six hundred natives, to whom she taught reading, writing, religion, and mechanical and agricultural arts. When in 1838 they were solemnly freed, a sum of money, a piece of land, and a cottage were waiting for each family—arranged for by Anne Marie. Eventually all of Mana became a free colony under her supervision and the Negroes gained the right to elect their delegate to the French Parliament. To a man they cast their votes for Mother Javouhey. When it was explained that a woman could not sit for them, they refused to cast a ballot at all.

Militant feminists would have disapproved of such slighting of women. Mother Javouhey no doubt merely smiled. She knew better than most how little sex mattered when it came to important affairs. Had she not accomplished what men had found impossible?

She was only one of a long tradition. The peculiar genius which is sanctity has for two thousand years been finding an outlet for its energies. She and hundreds of abbesses and prioresses and queens and peasant-saints had spent their lives proving that compassion and kindness, as well as greatness, are the special prerogatives of neither sex.

No influential women before the eighteenth century? Again, nonsense! There have been towering women since the world was invented. In order to be great one does not have to be a poet or a painter or a warrior or a discoverer of planets. One need only be a magnificent soul.

Holy Wit

Pre-Renaissance artists who had never studied anatomy used to paint their subjects as if they were quite boneless under the bright clothes. Pious writers have been in the habit of doing the same thing to saints, drawing them all soul and no body. They forget that what a reader wants is not a picture but a motion picture. The stir of life is missing, and so is the sound of a natural voice—the sigh of failure, the murmur of discontent, the ripple of human laughter. Most of all one misses the laughter.

Yet I am certain it is there. The dedicated saint-watcher, if he listens long enough, can hear it all about him, a delicate tintinnabulation of joyousness as old as sainthood. In forests of virtue the very branches quiver with gentle hilarity. And staring, one sees the saints shake off their carven poses and begin to move merrily like men and women. Ignatius Loyola flings up his arms, clicks his heels, and breaks into the Basque national dance to cheer his guest, the melancholy Ortiz. The Poor Clares warble through cloister halls. Francis of Assisi, carried away with pure happiness, holds a stick to one shoulder, draws another stick like a bow across his imaginary violin, and, so accompanied, carols "songs in the French tongue."

I have read that during the process of canonization the Catholic Church demands proof of joy in the candidate, and although I have not been able to track down chapter and verse I like the suggestion that dourness is not a sacred attribute. It is a pity hagiographers have not kept it more in mind.

The one kind of wit they are willing to grant their saints is the parting shot, as if good temper were admissible only on one's deathbed. I collect such mots gladly, since deathbed jokes are better than no jokes at all. I admire the ladylike nonchalance of Mary Mazzarello, who bantered with the priest who was giving her the last rites. When he had finished anointing her she looked up and said tartly, "Well, that's my passport. I expect I can leave any time, now."

I find it debonair of John Berchmans to mock the doctor's prescription for his illness. And indeed it does sound odd to modern ears since it consisted of bathing the patient's forehead with vintage wine. "A good thing I haven't long to live!" John muttered. "I can't afford such an expensive disease." Oscar Wilde said it better when he made his famous last quip, "I am dying as I lived, beyond my means." But John had not spent a lifetime studying the art of repartee.

And there is always the raillery of Sir Thomas More to add to an anthology of last words. More, "the most virtuous fellow in England," was a good family man, a good friend to Erasmus and all the wits of his day, and "the king's good servant but God's, first." (It was the final reservation that lost him his head.) He managed to be gay even to the executioner. "Assist me up, if you please," he said with as much aplomb as if he were still in his own drawing room. "Coming down I can shift for myself."

Surely saints who can respond to death in such fashion must also have owned gaiety in their lives. It takes patience to chip away at the plaster statue and release the merry human being, but it can be done. There is, for instance, Paschal Baylon, praised chiefly for his mortifications, at whom we can peek when he is being mirthful as a child with a kite. There he capers in the dining room where he is supposed to be laying the table—innocently dancing like another Juggler of Notre Dame jigging for joy before the Virgin's statue.

And now and then one comes across a character so ebullient that it cannot be stifled by the dreariest historian. Teresa of Avila, irrepressible as a volcano, unsinkable as balsa wood, never fitted for a moment into a pious straitjacket. "From silly devotions and sour-faced saints, good Lord deliver us!" she protested. And the salt of wit flavors her every action. Besides, she wrote letters endlessly, so her true voice comes through—praising, admonishing, or encouraging, but always with humor. We have her own description of the saint who was her right hand in reforming the Carmelite Order grown so lax and luxurious in Spain—the great John of the Cross. John was a tiny man, not five feet tall. Teresa valued him from the beginning when he became second of the two friars who rushed to her side when she was starting her difficult work. But she couldn't resist making fun of his size. "Isn't it splendid?" she wrote to a friend. "With John here, we now have a monk and a half."

Teresa could not live with pomposity. Self-importance was a balloon she pricked whenever she saw it bobbing along. I relish her advice to a young nun who came to her with tales of exaggerated temptation and who boasted of being a great sinner. "Now, Sister," Teresa said deflatingly, "remember, none of us are perfect. Just make sure those sins of yours don't turn into bad habits."

Literary pomposity annoyed her as much as any other kind. After reading some fatuous religious essay by a certain Señor Salcedo, she commented, "The man never stops repeating 'As Saint Paul says,' 'As the Holy Spirit says,' and then he ends by regretting that he has written nothing but nonsense. I am going to denounce him to the Inquisition."

The Inquisition was always a cloud on her horizon. Only superb tact kept her from actually falling into its bad graces. Ignatius was not so lucky and became its frequent scapegoat. He was once arrested for street-preaching and the solemnest of the Inquisitors was sent to examine him. "You are accused of teaching novelties," said the Father. "What have you to say for yourself?" "My Lord," answered Ignatius smoothly, "I should not have thought it had been any novelty to speak of Christ to Christians."

The Basques have a reputation for being taciturn, dry as Vermonters, and Ignatius was a Basque. But he had his own kind of humor and approved of happiness. Like John of Saxony, the good Dominican who said to the novices he found giggling in the seminary, "Keep on laughing, youngsters; it's the way you escape from the Devil," Ignatius commended *his* seminarians for gaiety. "Laugh and grow strong," he told them; and he advised sports as well as lessons for them, quite an innovation at a time when students at the Paris colleges were accustomed to rising at five in the morning, studying until nine before they so much as took breakfast, and going on with their books until candles guttered in the evening.

The Ignatian recreation seems to have been billiards, and one finds him playing once for a wager. A gentleman who was half thinking of turning Jesuit but balked at trying the Spiritual Exercises which were the first step on the journey, dined with him one day. After dinner Ignatius challenged him to a game. "If I lose, I shall become your servant for a month. If I win, you'll take a month for the Exercises."

One is glad to report that the saint beat his friend roundly.

He also enjoyed chess, as did Charles Borromeo. The latter was once criticized for the pleasure he took in his skill. "And what would you do if you were playing away and the end of the world suddenly arrived?" "Keep on playing chess," said Borromeo.

The steely Charles was an abstracted character, and it is not usual to see him in so light a mood. But then he lived in a dark time, almost as dark as ours. The Reformation had split the world apart. Borromeo had not only to repair its ravages in Italy but to try to root out its causes by reforming his own clergy. It did not leave him much time for games.

An occasional saint was so jocular that even the Reformation could not dim his good cheer. The most renowned of these was Philip Neri, who along with Borromeo, Pius V, and Loyola stands as one of the four pillars shouldering the sky when it seemed to be crashing over Europe. By eloquence and personal example they managed to rebuild, reinforce, and shore up religion's foundations, eaten away by corruption.

It's odd about Philip, though. He was so virtuous that the world sanctified him in his lifetime and so genial that the two books he valued most, as we have seen, were a New Testament and a volume of jokes and riddles. The Lives insist he was a wit, but his biographers seem to have strained out the witticisms and left us only his strange capers. His jokes seem practical jokes, his liveliness mere antics, like shaving half his beard and pretending to be tipsy by way of scotching rumors of his holiness. Still, we do know he was the least sour of men and believed like Ludovic Pavone (born delightfully on April Fool's Day) that "Rigorism keeps heaven empty."

"I will have no sadness in my house," he told the young men who flocked to his Oratory. And he was tirelessly kind to penitents. "Don't be forever dwelling on your sins," he advised them. "Leave a little something for the angels."

Leaving something for angels is one point on which he might have agreed with his mighty opponent Martin Luther. Master Martin's close friend was Philipp Melanchthon, author of the Augsburg Confessions. Melanchthon was a cool man where Luther was fervid, a scholar as opposed to a doer, and he continued to live like a monk even after he had joined the German Reformation and left off wearing the tonsure. One day Luther lost patience with Melanchthon's virtuous reserve. "For heaven's sake," he roared, "why don't you go out and sin a little? God deserves to have *something* to forgive you for!"

Humor in reformers always seems to me the dearest of

qualities and not common enough to this day. They tell us
Don John Bosco is celebrated for it, but he is like Philip
Neri in having had the essential juice somehow squeezed
out of him by historians. He, too, was patron to delinquent
boys and, three hundred years after Neri, used Nerian
techniques to rescue the homeless and hapless young of
Rome. (His boys adored him, and it is touching to read
that one of them, turning a lathe in some factory while
John passed by on the pavement, was so eager to reach
him that he plunged through the shop door, glass pane and
all.) He loved picnics, acrobatics, and "the civilizing effects
of good music." Yet, while he is called a wit, I find in him
chiefly a peasant's rough and ready good nature, perfectly suited to the juvenile mind. And his most famous
joke is a clown's joke, a Chaplinesque episode.

He had his foes, as reformers will, and they were strong
enough to persuade the authorities that the man was a
lunatic for trying to take charge of so great a group of
children without visible resources. In fact, a carriage arrived one day with two priests in it, prepared to carry him
off for examination at the hospital. John, however, had
been warned. So he was amiable to the fathers and said,
certainly, he would be happy to go with them "for a drive
in the country." He got his hat and coat, prepared to
step into the carriage, then suddenly seemed to remember
his manners. "After you, Fathers," he said with a flourish.
The two priests seated themselves, whereupon John
stepped back and slammed the door smartly, shouting to
the driver, "To the asylum." And the carriage rattled away
without him.

The peasant, however, could turn a neat phrase when
he needed it. "And what sort of habit have you designed
for your Order?" asked a literal-minded benefactor, when
John was attempting not to found the Salesians, which
later became a community, but simply to rent a building
where he could house his strays. "Why, the habit of virtue,
sir," said Don John.

It takes a good deal of eavesdropping and reading be-

tween the lines, though, to get at most of the gaiety. We
hear that Deicelus "was always smiling" or that Lioba
"had a face like an angel, ever pleasant and laughing,"
but one can only guess at the humor behind the wonder-
working. And sometimes saints are witty simply by accident. I find it amusing that Good King Wenceslaus of the
ballad is listed in the calendar along with his daughter. I
think it diverting that Saint Vitus is patron not of the dance
but of those who, like me, have trouble getting up early
in the morning; and that Benedict of Amiane began his
career as cupbearer to Charlemagne. Indeed, it seems to
me comic that Charlemagne himself was long ago beatified. What heaven makes of that warlike and half-pagan
old conqueror one can only surmise. But he won the title
of "Blessed" long before canonization became an official
Church function and when it was a shabby hero or an
amazingly incompetent bishop who did not make the lists
by local acclaim once he was safely dead.

For that matter, the great Jerome often seems uneasy
among the holy congregation. A fiercer man never lived to
drive the Desert Fathers mad with argument. Yet no one
can deny his wit. It was wit of a deadly brand, killing as
a sword. One sees it at work in his letters to Augustine,
himself no mean opponent. He uses it as a weapon against
heresy, the heresy which often seems to be any doctrine
with which Jerome did not agree. Poor Rufinus, once the
friend whom Jerome almost hysterically adulated, lives
forever pilloried in the screed the fiery doctor wrote
against him when they disputed over the theories of Origen. Jerome not only demolished Rufinus's case, he demolished Rufinus. He describes the poor fellow's "tortoise
walk," the way he cracked his fingers and beamed when
he was about to make a telling point for an audience, his
little grunts and hiccoughs and classroom mannerisms. It
is a cruel portrait and about as saintlike a job as one of
Swift's satires.

Still, there is another side to Jerome, when the old lion
turns gentler and merely smiles at another saint, Fabiola,

whose nature was so sociable that she could not bear to be without company. "Her idea of the stable is that it should be an annex to the inn," he says with perfect good temper, and we begin to see why men might have been willing to follow him to the wilderness.

Nearly as sociable as Fabiola was Pius X, although as Pope in the restless nineteenth century he had little enough time to indulge that side of his sunny nature. He did make one endearing innovation as soon as he came to the Vatican. It had been a long-standing custom there that popes took their meals alone. Pius would have none of the stately tradition. He dined with his relatives, with friends, and visiting priests; he ate with messengers, aides, the workmen in his gardens. Not even the crushing weight of the tiara could quench his gregariousness. What did quench it for a time was hearing that people had begun to call him a saint and were counting up his miracles. "So now it's miracles they want from me," he burst out. "As if I didn't have enough to do already!"

Pius belongs to our modern age, so he is not hard to spy on. As a saint-watcher, though, I find the sport more exhilarating when I can come across some unexpected flash of color in a somber copse, or catch a small domestic glimpse of holy people at play. I enjoy listening to the comment of the Little Poor Man who, after lodging for a while at the house of a certain Cardinal Leo, went home and caught an ague so painful that he swore he had been beaten by the Devil. "Which is my punishment," said Francis, "for consorting with Cardinals."

I cherish the little scene at table with Thomas More— the same Thomas who contrived a joke with his executioner. More had trained for sainthood long before he fell into the bad graces of Henry VIII, and always practiced secret austerities. The secret came out one day at dinner with his family. He had taken off his ruff for comfort, when, eyeing him, his daughter-in-law fell into a fit of giggles. As the rest of the company followed her pointing finger, they caught the hysteria. More looked down at himself and began to laugh as loudly as they. Then he hastily and shamefacedly stuffed back under his doublet the secret hairshirt that had been nudging itself into sight.

I love his brand of unself-conscious piety as I admire Madeleine Sophie Barat's retort to a disapproving letter. Madeleine Sophie was a great teacher, a great lady, and a Frenchwoman to the bone. She founded the Society of the Sacred Heart, and the Madames of that aristocratic order still educate young women all over the world. (The present Crown Princess of Japan was once a Sacred Heart pupil in Tokyo, and I would lay a small bet that to this day she remembers how to curtsy on a staircase with a load of books in her arms as well as she knows how to conjugate a Latin verb. The curtsy is a Sacred Heart specialty along with the classics.) Mother Barat lived before Jane Austen, but there is a touch of Austen in her tone when she rebukes the popinjay who had suggested resentfully that French girls in her schools were aping the curriculum reserved for French gentlemen. "Our Society," she wrote, "has not been established to prove that women can become men, even though that may be easy in a country where so many men become women."

The female saints seem often to be sharper-mannered than the men; or perhaps they are merely franker in their letters. I discover male saints so incapable of malice that one wonders how they managed to survive in this imperfect world. John of Vercelli found it impossible to frown and had to insist that his "socius," or aide in the Dominican Order, should be "of severe and awe-inspiring countenance." Antony Grassi could not bear to hear an angry syllable. "Please, Father," he used to beg the prior, "only a few inches of voice." It was the same Antony who, struck by lightning, claimed cheerfully that the bolt had cured him of indigestion, a remedy one can scarcely recommend.

But when I am searching for the elusive accent of wit, I can always return to Avilan Teresa, who never fails me. Mystic that she was, she lived in such astonishing communication with God that they carried on conversations—where God sometimes sounds very much like Teresa. I have quoted her most famous comment earlier; not so familiar is the scrap of dialogue she records at a time when one of her recalcitrant abbesses was being particularly tiresome. "Lord," she prayed, "if I had my way that woman wouldn't be Superior here." And God answered her as wryly. "Teresa," He said, "if I had My way, she wouldn't be, either."

Overhearing, I am reassured. Wit is not the prerogative of the unjust, and there is truly laughter in holy places.

❀

Saints by Nationality

Three against the Grain

All saints, as I said at the beginning, do not suit all tastes. The watcher, if he is not to retire disgruntled from his occupation, must retain a tolerant mind. For every Francis Xavier, irresistibly lovable, there is an icy Borromeo to whom it is difficult to give one's affection. Each endearing Lioba has her formidable counterpart—some abbess or head of a convent, such, say, as America's own Mother Cabrini, who seems to have been canonized as much for her business acumen as for her holiness. What the dilettante must remember is that the saints who appeal least to us in this odd segment of the twentieth century possessed traits highly prized in their own era or in their particular part of the world. The environment, the need, produced the person rather than the other way around.

I think now of Bernard of Clairvaux, mighty voice of the twelfth century. The triumphs which made him celebrated in his day have little relevance to ours. Crusader, ascetic, scourge of heretics, he looms from this distance a figure in no way agreeable. For one thing, he preached war, and the fact that it appeared to him a holy war does not surround his mission with extra radiance. One must transport oneself to the climate of those times to understand why his brand of zealotry fired the Western nations.

The very existence of Christian civilization then seemed

imperiled. Islam strode victorious in the East and was thrusting westward. By Christmas Day, 1144, the Turks had captured Edessa, center of one of the four "principalities of the Latin Kingdom of Jerusalem." To the fervent it looked like the end of the world. Jerusalem was their Mecca. Even at the cost of battle it must be returned, they thought, to the Christian community. Dying for the faith was a way of salvation, and if they took some equally ardent Moslems along with them, they believed it all in a good cause.

So when Bernard shook the mountains with his eloquence, he stirred a continent. Off to the Second Crusade went Louis VII of France (himself a failed saint) and his Amazonian consort, Eleanor of Aquitaine. Along with them rode as many Franks and Burgundians and other European knights as could raise a regiment or equip a company. If some rode for loot as well as for God and glory, such motives are the same in all crusades.

Bernard's God must not have approved the war, for it was one of the great disasters of a disastrous time. French and Frankish troops were turned back with enormous loss, after having done little more than besiege Damascus for a brief, humiliating period. Moreover, one can derive amusement of a grim sort on learning what happened to the seven thousand foot soldiers Louis left behind him in Satalia when he was cut off from his supplies and forced to return, defeated, to France. Surrounded on one side by supposedly Christian Greeks, and on the other by the Turks, those warriors realistically surveyed their situation. The Greeks, they decided, were the more bloodthirsty. So seven thousand Crusaders who for the sake of their souls had sought to liberate the Holy Land from unbelievers, for the sake of their bodies embraced Islam. It is a plot for today's black humorists.

Nor does Bernard in his role as abbot sound any more delightful at first glance. His monastery rule was so rigorous that he himself had to moderate it lest his monks die off from starvation and overwork. He hounded the

Albigensians with the same harshness that led him to excommunicate the flies of his parish church. And it was he who brought down the career of his most brilliant adversary, a man as learned as himself, Peter Abelard.

Yet he has been eternally admired. To this day men interested in the meditative life, even one so modern in his thinking as the late Thomas Merton, have taken Bernard as patron. He has remained a torch for all ages. Erasmus, no lover of asceticism, four centuries after the saint's death, was praising him as "cheerful, pleasant, and vehement in moving the passions." And his own era adored him. He embodied twelfth-century aspirations, was the prop and support of all that seemed best to citizens of the late Middle Ages.

It was a strange time, as most times seem strange to those who come afterward. Europe seemed threatened on every hand with infidels at its gates, unrest and heresy at home. The Papacy, which had for long been a unifying element, was falling captive to both the state and its own corruption. Bernard fought all the dangers in sight. If he singled out the Albigensians to preach against most ardently (and he preached only; the military war against them came a century later in a more enlightened and crueler age) it was because their peculiar doctrines seemed destructive to the world's morality.

They *were* a quirky, immoderate people. Actually they were not Christians at all but a sect deriving from sources that had troubled the Church since Pauline days. They drew strength from that Manichean spring which had never ceased to flow—from the first apostates, who had taught that all fleshly things were evil, that the body was the creation of the Devil, and that the Christ who had been martyred on the cross could not be their Christ since God could not die. This belief led to some curious practices. If the body was evil, it did not matter to the soul what the body did. Marriage, like all other innocent merriments, was denied the Elect. The pure must have no truck with sensual things, and even procreation was forbidden them. But Albigensians were human beings, so their human lapses in sexual matters outside marriage gave rise to great scandal. They themselves had found a way around such salvation-denying behavior. Only the truly Saved could get to Heaven. So they were in the habit of waiting until they were on their deathbeds to receive the sacraments, thus walking into Paradise without stain. Their customs may seem to us merely quaint. To Bernard's generation they constituted a grave disruption of the peace, particularly since they were making converts rapidly.

Yet Bernard must have had just a touch of the Albigensian in himself—so does any virus one fights turn infectious —for he, too, believed that in order to remain virtuous one ought to insulate oneself from a sinful world. Perhaps his natural endowments made him wary of that world. He belonged to the Burgundian nobility, a class never celebrated for its own moderation. He was handsome, witty, gifted, therefore (he felt) quite capable of being pulled into the dissolute whirlpools yawning for people of his age and station. So when he decided to become a religious, he took to his form of desert, turning his back on society not because it was evil *per se* but because it had too much attraction for him.

His was the twelfth-century point of view. Heretics there may have been then, but few atheists. And to true believers of whatever persuasion the God of the Middle Ages was a jealous, implacable Jehovah. Man forever creates deities in his own image. In Bernard's time, the gentleness of the New Testament had been partially replaced by the strictures of the Old. Heaven may have been a longed-for spot, but hell was more real than any other prospect. It gaped horridly for sinners just over the hill from death; and Bernard, like his contemporaries, thought of life as merely an interlude between birth and judgment. There were humanists teaching then but few humanitarians. Although Bernard pitied the poor and deplored the cruelties of overlords, it would never have occurred to him to attempt to alter the structure of society.

Providence had placed each man in his ordained station as serf, noble, or king; it was incumbent on him to perform with virtue and patience the duties of his office, not to topple the feudal concept. Saving one's soul rather than reforming politics was the business of Everyman.

That was best accomplished, people everywhere held, by prayer and penance. So Bernard's resolve to become a Cistercian monk was as natural then as it would be now for an idealistic young man to fling his energies into rebuilding a slum or joining the Peace Corps. But it must not have been an easy decision. To give up an advantaged world in which he fitted so pleasantly, in which he was already making a name for himself as writer and cavalier, must have been wrenching. But once he had chosen a destiny, his bent for enthusiastic leadership came into play. Not only did he set out for the severest of monasteries, the strict enclosure at Cîteaux headed by the Englishman who was to become Saint Stephen, but he carried along with him by sheer force of personality thirty-one mesmerized companions, including an uncle and four of his brothers. Butler, with unusual emotion, has described Bernard's later impact on worldly society when his wheedling tongue brought men pouring into his abbeys. "Mothers feared for their sons," he writes, "wives for their husbands, lest they come under the sway of that compelling voice and look."

And well they might, for nobody of his day seems to have been able to resist him. They could not do so when he was merely a twenty-two-year-old novice. As he was leaving home, the tale runs, he went for a final goodby to his father, Tescalin, and the youngest of the family, Nivard. Bernard, as a good son, had told Nivard he must stay to comfort Tescalin and manage the family properties.

"Adieu, my little Nivard," he said at parting. "You will have all the estates and lands for yourself."

But Nivard had listened too well to Bernard. "What!" he cried. "You then take heaven and leave me only the earth?" It was more than the boy could bear, and shortly afterward not only he but Tescalin also went to join their family Pied Piper.

Only a sister, Humbaline, remained in the world, disapproving of the whole project. "I prefer dancing to devotions," she said honestly. But there was more than honesty in her; there was resentment, too. She took what must have been malicious delight in taunting Bernard to his face with her frivolity when she could persuade him to a meeting. She was in the habit of dressing herself up as giddily as possible, then, in her silks and furs and riding with a group of noisy companions, appearing at the monastery gates.

He won out, however, in the end. Eventually Humbaline herself went to a convent and turned so virtuous that she is now listed as "Blessed" in the Calendar. To convert a continent seems to me less astonishing than reforming one's own family. But then Bernard was a genius. The fact that he intimidates us does not detract from his greatness. Also, when one knows the truth, he is not so very frightening after all. His "persecution" of heretics was only a form of persuasion, since words rather than swords were his weapons.

As for the Crusade, that was preached at the command of the Pope. And if Bernard ruined the unfortunate Abelard, it was done by argument, not force; nor could he have achieved such total victory except for the impediment in Abelard's own nature.

Even Bernard's (to us) excessive austerities were merely part and parcel of twelfth-century practice. Moreover, as he grew wiser with age, he modified them for both himself and his community. Whether or not we can love him, he is undeniably a transcendent figure. By the example of his life he reformed France; by his efforts he reformed the Papacy—at least for the time being. And he left for all ages a body of spiritual writing so sweet and so exalted that it has comforted believing mankind for eight hundred years.

However distant Bernard seems, he is far closer to us

than such a figure as Rose of Lima, who lived in the less remote sixteenth century. For at least he was an authentic hero and scholar who, in spite of his rigorous religious convictions, had a good deal of common sense. He was also a European, shaped by European thought. Rose was Spanish by descent but Peruvian by birth, and in her the two fanatic strains merged to form a wild, nearly incredible brand of sanctity understandable only to the people of her own nation.

A bald recital of her life as recorded by hagiographers horrifies our modern senses, rationalists and activists that we are. She wore a crown of thorns. She scarred her face with pepper so no man would find her attractive. Someone had the bad taste to praise her hands, so she dipped them into lye. She set up housekeeping in a hut in the family garden and ate no food except the most meager and unappetizing. She died at thirty-one, and no wonder; the marvel is that she managed to last so long, considering her many illnesses and the bad treatment she chose to inflict on herself. If she had ever been a sinner, one might make allowances for the punishments, since sin aches for repentance. But, unless one counts as a mortal fault her refusal to marry as her parents wished, those austerities lack rational basis. From the cradle (at least according to the biographers) she lived a dedicated and blameless life.

As for her accomplishments, they seem few. It is true that when her family fell on hard times she helped support them by gardening and fine sewing. And it is also said that frivolous society in Lima got into the habit of consulting her for advice on "devout behavior." But unlike Catherine of Siena, who was her heroine, Rose effected few reforms and had little impact on politics or religion.

Yet she, too, was the idol of her day. When she died her casket was carried to the grave by all the heads of the city, each group of notables taking turns as bearers. As the coffin passed, surging crowds hysterically snatched at it, seizing pieces of her shroud, the flowers on the bier, even slivers of the casket to take home as relics. No dead movie star now could produce such a spontaneous outburst of adulation. And she received canonization more rapidly than almost any saint in the Calendar.

Is there anything that can explain her to us now? Only, I think, the circumstances of her nationality and the time in which she attempted holiness. Still, those may be enough, since sanctity flowers to fill a local need, a seasonal demand.

Her season was the fervent spring of the late Reformation. And her climate was that of a new wilderness, a Spanish civilization thinly laid over Indian culture, one as conducive to ascetic excess as fourth-century Antioch. In fact, without some knowledge of Peruvian history we cannot see Rose in context at all. Although the story may be familiar, it is worth retelling.

Only about fifty years before her birth in 1586, Pizarro with his vest-pocket army had overrun the ancient empire of the Incas at the exact moment it was ripe for conquest. It was no mean state he encountered. Its capital was Cuzco but the Incan government extended over much of South America as far south as Chile and was as formal and ritualized as antique Egypt, which it in some ways resembled. All power centered in the king; the state was responsible for the welfare of all its subjects and owned everything except houses and "moveable household goods." There were taxes. There were roads and great engineering projects, irrigation and drainage, arts, crafts, and a highly systematized religion. But in the sixteenth century something had happened to the country which was as tragic as it was romantic.

The Emperor Huayna Capac, attempting to extend the borders of his rule, took title to the province of Quito. Although he met little military opposition, Quito, in the person of its princess, conquered him. He fell deeply in love and the pair had a son named Atahualpa. Although Huayna already had an heir by legitimate marriage to his sister (which was the connubial pattern of Incan kings) he was so besotted by affection for his princess that he made the one mistake no dynast can afford: he divided his realm between the true prince, Huascar, and his beloved Atahualpa. Once the Emperor was dead, Atahualpa challenged his half-brother for the whole imperial prize, and the result was a civil war in which Atahualpa emerged both victor and victim. For the country, used to a peaceful, monolithic reign, had fallen into confusion. At the moment of its weakness, Pizarro burst into the mountains with his less than three hundred soldiers. But the few had guns against spears. They rode horses, which the Indians had never seen. They knew the tactics of surprise. They also had as protection a legend very old in the Incan religion, one native both to Peru and to Mexico—a story of white gods who had once ruled over the land and who would come again in time of trouble. No anthropologist has been able to find how the rumor originated. Some think that westward-faring Celtic monks had once reached that kingdom and preached Christian doctrine to the Indians. The newest surmise is that the Phoenicians long before Christ landed there and brought Mediterranean customs with them. The fabled deities might even have been missionaries from Asia. At any rate, the myth was so deeply entrenched in Peruvian minds that even Atahualpa welcomed the Spanish as if they were angels.

No army, of course, could have been less angelic. Of the many conquistadors, Pizarro was the most ruthless, a bold and brilliant soldier but a rough opportunist who could neither read nor write. His progress through the country, however, from the coast to the mountains, was one of the amazing exploits of all time. He was coming, he told the populace, as ambassador from a friendly monarch. He brought gifts to the chiefs, spoke of friendship and amity. And he was entirely successful. These were pacific subjects of a government which had never encouraged initiative. There were no local firebrands to raise a rebellion in the countryside. Nor was there opposition even at court when Pizarro and Atahualpa met at Caxamarca. The Incan king, himself a crafty, even unscrupulous warrior, seems to have been suspicious but uncharacteristically indecisive. He accepted the trumpery gifts, admired the strangers' horses. He received and fed the Spanish and let them lodge in one of the public buildings. Perhaps it was a ruse. He may have been turning over in his mind the simplest way of taking the invaders captive. If so, he waited too long, for Pizarro, surrounded by genuine armies, thousands of Indians all obedient to their leader, knew he had only one route to military victory. He must, as Prescott puts it, "secure the person of the Indian prince."

Schoolbooks repeatedly tell the story from this point on —how Atahualpa came with his courtiers to Pizarro's camp, how the conquistador first asked his guest to surrender to the King of Spain and to accept the Spanish religion, how, when he quite naturally refused, Pizarro's soldiers opened fire and very nearly demolished the city, taking Atahualpa as hostage. Then followed the famous episode of Pizarro's outrageous demand for ransom—a roomful of gold from the Incas in return for the liberty of their sovereign. What is more, Atahualpa's followers actually did produce the room filled with gold, although they might have wondered why the strangers so much desired a commodity which, since the Indians had not yet learned to work in iron, was the domestic metal of the kingdom. But in spite of the achieved ransom Atahualpa was put to death on a charge of conspiring with his chiefs to overturn the Spanish occupation. Pizarro could not afford to let so powerful a man, by now his outright foe, loose among the people.

Gentler Huascar was already dead, assassinated by his ambitious brother. The empire was leaderless. Into that vacuum the Spaniards moved, and by the middle of the century nearly the whole of South America was, at least in name, a part of Spain's extraordinary colonies. Stolidly the Indians accepted the new rule. Since they had always been reigned over by authority-at-a-distance, the masses did not expect things to be much different from before.

Fate had simply put over them the white man instead of their former Sun King. And just as passively they accepted the outward aspects of the new religion.

Lima was established early as an important city. Treasure-hunters arrived. Spain sent over administrators and clergy, and along with them came adventurers, artisans, even a few planters. Lima, trying to ignore its Indians, became superficially a Spanish town. But such a country as Peru always absorbs its conquerors, and slowly, insidiously, the apparently quenched Incan culture made itself felt, altering religious concepts, imposing its strange aura on society. The Christianity of the natives was no more than a veneer over old beliefs and primitive superstitions. Having always been fatalists, they understood the cult of suffering better than they did that of the Resurrection. (The same was true of Mexico, where to this day the Flagellants and the Penitentes flourish, if only underground.) No matter how shadowy their influence on a Latin culture, it existed.

It is against this background the watcher must observe Rose. Hers was the mind of the mystic. But it was bound to be swayed by her frontier environment, certain to be seduced by the faintly heard but constant voice of submerged Indian multitudes. Besides, she was a true innocent and romantic who no doubt had been brought up on tales of ascetic saints that peopled the childhood romances of the time.

After all, what was the most popular reading matter in devout households, then, even in England and Puritan America? What kind of literary fare did small children receive to mold their characters? It was Foxe's *Book of Martyrs,* and no grislier tome has ever chilled the blood of a juvenile. Again, this was the Reformation era, one which remembered blood and judgment. So a less fiercely ascetic holy woman would not have appealed to Lima. Martin de Porres, her charming contemporary, is *our* kind of hero, a genuine Assisian, gentle, mild, charitable. He worked far more miracles of love in Lima than did Rose.

But for generations he remained only beatified, and it was not until recently that he was elevated to a full halo. Without the fasts, trances, and apparitions, the bed of shards, and the hairshirt, he did not cry out to the Lima citizenry with so authentic a note. He was not singular enough to suit his epoch.

But what did Rose *accomplish?* we ask ourselves now. One must turn to the early biographers for the answer if there is to be one.

I grant them one virtue in Rose's case. They made no attempt to attribute to her the noble lineage with which they dearly love to endow their subjects. "Her family," comments Butler, "were decent folk of moderate means." This implies that they descended from the stock of treasure-seekers who had never struck it rich. We know that Rose's father, Caspar, lost what money he had in a mining venture and that Rose then took to truck farming and embroidery. But since they were of undiluted Spanish blood the De Flores family kept caste. And Marie de Flores, like any normal mother, had ambitions for her daughter who was, according to the stories, a genuine beauty. Maria wanted to marry off her pretty Rose to a young grandee, or at least to Lima's equivalent of a grandee.

Yes, she knew the child had made a vow to be "Christ's bride or none," but what mother believes the fancies of an attractive adolescent? The child would grow out of such ridiculous notions. So she dragged Rose about from party to party, hoping for the best. Personally, my sympathy goes to Maria. How can a domestic fowl understand the behavior of the eagle or the swan it has unwittingly hatched? And what else can the mystified hen do but cluck distractedly over its unusual offspring until the fledgling escapes alone into its natural element?

Rose had no Dr. Spock on her side to advise rebellion, no flower child to emulate by running away. Desperately trying to thwart her mother's plans for a secular vocation, she resorted to the pepper, the lye. Evidently she found physical pain an aid to spiritual concentration. Out of innocence of any other method, she made it a ladder on which to climb. Finally Maria, worn out by her daughter's stubbornness, gave up the struggle and allowed Rose first to build her garden hut, then to fast as she wished, and to go her own eccentric way. In the tiny shelter the girl mapped out a systematic pattern for her chosen martyrdom, which seems to us so eerie. For twelve hours of the day she prayed. For ten she worked. She slept for two. Besides the hairshirt, she wore a chain belt, designed to cut into her flesh. When her confessor insisted on shortening the thorns in her little silver crown, she simply dug the prongs deeper into her head. No one was strong enough to stand against her.

At length her confidence in her vocation grew sufficiently firm so that she left her hermitage from time to time to go into the hospitals and nurse the sick poor, comfort prostitutes, become a public symbol of virtue. And it is true that she had such influence on the townspeople of Lima that they gentled their conduct and took their religion more seriously.

Yet other saints, by the hundreds, have done far more. Her importance lies in the fact that she translated the hybrid passions of frontier Peru into something both the Spaniards and the Indians could comprehend. Violent societies need violent images to arouse them. Rose gave the Western Hemisphere a spiritual identity.

So it is possible for us to offer her a full salute even if we cannot give her our hearts. She spoke to her time and her people. And her Lord, who is conceded to be as tender as He is just, probably welcomed her into Paradise with a ready gesture. "Make yourself at home, dear child," one can imagine Him saying. "In your own curious manner you tried to join yourself with Me and none who seek Me will I turn away."

It is even possible He said the same to Simeon Stylites when that mad pillar saint arrived at the end of his fantastic pilgrimage. But only a very tolerant God could really have received him with anything except amusement. For if Rose seems excessive and Bernard stern, they were both more or less reasonable figures. Simeon, by our standards, was a lunatic. "Even the Desert Fathers," says one historian, "were disgusted by his personal habits." And since the Desert Fathers on the whole were not temperate men, Simeon must have been indeed outrageous to set them looking askance at his behavior.

Even hagiography eyes him warily. "It must be acknowledged," Butler warns, "that his most remarkable actions are a subject of admiration, not of imitation."

Our century can find in him little enough to admire. He was born the son of a shepherd in Cilicia, on the borders of Syria, about 389. This was near enough to Antioch to come under the influence of those solitude-loving men we call the Desert Fathers although their "desert" was not a Sahara but a wilderness; sometimes no more than sparsely inhabited country. The Church was very Eastern then. Rome had had no chance to shape it into a Latin structure with codified rules and a real hierarchy, or to soften its anchoritic drive with European moderation. "Saints" of all descriptions were fleeing into caves and trees and wattled shelters to escape what they believed to be the contamination of libertine cities. Simeon was only the most notorious of them. And he began his austerities early. At thirteen, the books tell us, "he was much moved by hearing the Beatitudes one day read in church, particularly the words, 'Blessed are they that mourn; blessed are the clean of heart.'"

That sanctity must rejoice had not yet become a tenet in the process of canonization. As we know, there was as yet no legal process. Saints were simply acclaimed by popular consensus after their deaths, and very odd were some of the early people who got included in the lists. So the fact that Simeon went into penitential mourning for the rest of his life did not, in that time, write him off the slate. But what barbarous penances they were that he invented!

First he spent several months as servant in a monastery,

"where he learned the psalter by heart" and "practiced the austerities of the house." But the monks there were not severe enough for him, so he went on to another, stricter enclosure. Even that place found him too fanatic for their approved methods. When the abbot discovered that the boy had tied a rope of twisted palm leaves about his waist until it cut so deep a gash that it could scarcely be removed, he dismissed his novice with a "warning to the rest to avoid such dangerous singularities."

After that, Simeon wandered about for a while, roving from abbey to abbey, in search of some institution which would allow him to savage himself as he wished. He tried fasting for total Lent, chaining himself to a rock, standing for days at a time in furious prayer. It was hopeless. His appetite for punishment was forever being thwarted by some disapproving father or by the rule of a house. So he left community life behind him and began his career of living on a pillar. He was not the first eccentric to try the feat. Pillar-dwelling was rather a fad among hermits just then. Simeon was certainly, however, the most famous and persistent.

His first pillar he built himself near Antioch, and it is described as being "six cubits high," which means about five yards off the ground. On this he lived for four years. It was uncomfortable but not sufficiently so for his appetite, and he went on building or having built for him, by enthusiastic disciples, pillar after pillar (which is the English translation of "stylos," after which he took his name) until he got himself up into the air as high as forty cubits. And finally, there, on a platform six feet wide, and dressed in the skins of animals, he resided for twenty years more.

What did he do up there, exposed to all weathers, depending on the charity of pilgrims for his meals, almost too limited in the matter of space to lie or even sit easily? Well, he kept far busier than one could expect. He prayed, almost without ceasing. He bobbed about a great deal, kneeling and genuflecting with dervish-like frenzy. "A visitor," Butler writes, "once reckoned 1244 such profound reverences made by him at one time." Perhaps it was such ghostly calisthenics which kept him thriving for so long in spite of irregular food and lack of what we consider shelter.

And he preached with the fervor of an antique Billy Graham, to continually increasing outdoor congregations. At the start he may have been no more than a tourist attraction. Any exceptional solitary then was fairly certain to be visited. In those spectacle-starved days people went to stare at hermits as they might now come to Disneyland. But in the case of Simeon the tourists quickly turned into converts. There must have been something ferociously sincere about his homilies, as there was about his life. How he, who had spent his years since boyhood stamping out self-indulgence in himself, could know much about sinning or about the world is a puzzle. And in truth the topics for his sermons seem, from what reports we have of them, to have been less than sensational. He exhorted his audiences against "usury and injustice" but he kept his most ardent words for diatribes against "the horrible custom of swearing." Still, people continued to gather until they became multitudes.

He converted thousands—Arabs, Persians, Armenians, as well as the local inhabitants. He became an oracle. The Emperor Theodosius and Pope Leo I often "consulted him and desired his prayers." Marcian, another Emperor, visited him frequently "although in disguise." Even the ordained clergy, who might have been hostile, since a sensible hierarchy has always frowned on oddities, yielded to the popular *cultus* and gave him their own blessing. Antioch's Patriarch, Domnus, was in the habit of bringing him Holy Communion and sending it up in a basket to his pillar, as the pilgrims did the meals they fetched him. If he had his detractors, their voices were (like those of the disgusted Fathers I have mentioned) drowned out in the general adoration, which consistently increased until his death in 495.

For, strange figure that he was, and of a type which is

anathema to our generations, here is the thing we have to remember about him: he was exactly the kind of dedicated man that era demanded. This was Syria in the Near East, an Arab, almost an Oriental country. And for centuries the "fakir," the holy mad man, had been a prototype for sanctity in such regions. He would be recognized today in India, in Tibet, or Turkey. Even his native country might still give him homage. Singularity does not offend the non-Occidental mind. Not in spite of but *because* of his addiction to pillar-living, he became the foremost celebrity in his part of the world.

Other times, other customs. I, as saint-watcher, cannot be his apologist, since I find nothing in him beguiling. On the other hand, I dare not deny him his place in the galaxy. He, limited, literal, and illiterate, listened to what he thought of as the Word and followed it during his whole fanatic existence. He became his own monument, a very "pillar of cloud by day and of fire by night," announcing salvation to a people avid for his exaggerated message.

We can try to understand him by recognizing the phenomena that shaped him. In truth, we should be better able to communicate with him than he with us. He, and the other two of the trio, would find our age a complete enigma. By slashing through the underbrush of history we can view them plain, but they would have no such trails blazed for them. Our activism, our revolutionary tendencies, would make no sense.

Even the conduct of saints a century or two back would baffle them. What would Rose have made of such a peripatetic figure as Mother Javouhey—Rose, who would never so much as attend mass unless accompanied by her mother? How would Bernard have regarded a Don Bosco, a M. Vincent, those worldly apostles? And what would they have thought of our most modern candidate for sainthood, kind John XXIII, with his affection for heretics and unbelievers? Not, one suspects, very much.

As for what goes on now among avant-garde clergy, I think my three might shudder at the idea of short-skirted, guitar-playing nuns and priests in mufti leading picket lines or courting jail on behalf of the underprivileged. The one thing they might endorse is the hunger strike; but then it would be the act they admired, not the motive behind the act.

Yet I may be wrong. Virtue might be able to interpret virtue. Who knows? A Bernard living today and in touch with world problems might well be in the forefront of the battle against injustice. Rose's visions might beckon her into ghettos instead of to a hiding place. Even Simeon might find a less remote platform from which to preach against the planet's ills. His pillar might become a soapbox on a street corner rather than a stylos in the desert. And who am I, in any case, to detract from the splendor of any of the three, bizarre though it may seem? Each appealed to the sensibilities of the moment. Each was a *rara avis*, yet each matched his or her encasing century. We may reject them as friends but not as prophets. For as I once said in another connection, "It takes all kinds to make a heaven."

The Wine of the Country

It also takes all sorts to make a world.

Since saints are not supernatural creatures but products of that world—products also of a particular portion of it— by and large the grapes of their achievements taste of the local vineyards where their souls first took root.

Few of them are so formed by an epoch or a region as Simeon and Rose. Yet they do, for the most part and to change the figure, come indelibly stamped "Made in Italy" or Hungary or Spain or England. If ever Rome, cured of its odd myopia, looks across the Atlantic to select a truly native candidate, we will find our own saints no doubt combining holiness with indigenous Yankee know-how and recognize them at once to be as unmistakably American as Catherine of Siena, say, was Italian.

Powerful as she was (and in her brief day she was the most powerful woman in Europe), she was at base thoroughly a Latin. She might lecture popes, instruct kings, dominate emperors. Yet that very domination has about it the aura of the Italian mother. She is the sub-limated Sienese matriarch, alternately exhorting, com-manding, wheedling, and always expecting—and obtaining —obedience from her brood. Embraces follow scolding; her letters mingle baby talk with stern homilies. Writing to Pope Urban V at Avignon in her most formal tone, she suddenly breaks into an eloquent definition of papal duty to call him *"Babba mio."*

Her close little circle of poets and cavaliers and artists tried vainly to address her properly as Madame but could never get past an affectionate and familiar *"Mama."* Moreover, among them she was renowned, even while she herself fasted, for her excellent cooking. One suspects, too, that her obstinate refusal to let the popes live out of the country was motivated as much by her passionate love for Italian soil as by a conviction that Rome was strategically designed to house the Vatican.

So it goes with many of the procession. Francis de Sales, God's elegant courtier, is French to his fingertips. Ireland's fathers, as we shall see in a later chapter, are amusingly Gaelic. And rampaging Scandinavian saints served their Lord, or thought to serve him, with a typically Viking gesture.

Olaf, patron of Norway, is most famous of the northland's canonized; and appears to have been canonized as much for martial as for spiritual valor. Hagiography writes him down as "martyr," which merely means he did not die in bed. For he was killed in a battle trying to regain the territories from which his people, infuriated at his attempt to make Christians out of them overnight, had driven him forth. His chief defect as an apostle was not lack of conviction but lack of tact. He was, after all, a Norseman of the eleventh century, in his youth a raider and a pirate, and he had so lately exchanged Valhalla for the Christian heaven that the warrior in him had scarcely had time to be erased.

He wished to do two great things: to bring the Gospels to his countrymen and to fetch Norway into the community of Western Christendom. Both were admirable objectives. It was only his headlong Viking manners that were at fault. He forgot that the folk he wished to convert were as stubborn, as brave, as individualistic as he, and would resist any attempt at mass baptism. So he fell, as I say, in a battle after having vigorously begun the belated evangelization of Scandinavia.

The Middle Ages, always eager to sanctify a dead hero, made a legend out of Olaf. All sorts of miracles and wonders were reported about the place of his burial—a disease-healing spring which suddenly gushed from the hillside, marvels of conversions and answered prayers attributed to his shrine. His cult spread through all the North, to England and beyond. And, since mankind comes to little harm when it exalts an episode into a myth (if that myth soothes and spurs the soul), let us not begrudge him his laurels. Perhaps they were more deserved than they seem from this time and this vantage place in history.

Far more securely lodged with the blessed is such a saint as Albertus Magnus, the great Albert who is Germany's pride. Scientist, preacher, obedient friar, he honestly earned his aureole. But for all his achievements, secular and pious, he never quite eludes his nationality. The Dominican habit clothes a meticulous Germanic scholar, absorbed in note-taking, forever on the track of proof for his theories. He is almost a caricature of a Teutonic intellectual. Strip him of his robes, give him a pair of horned-rimmed glasses, put a camera in his hand, and we would recognize him today for what he essentially is— good, sedulous observer of the natural world.

Fortunately he came from Swabia. I say "fortunately" because the province of Swabia has given us its most happy examples of German genius. Even so late as the terrible forties of this century, these *gemütlich* people were proving their human mettle. Hitler visited them once at the peak of his triumphs. And how did they receive him? With boos and hisses, with an electric blackout, an interruption of the public-address system, and such open hostility that he never ventured back. Perhaps Albert's spirit has endowed his compatriots with a kind of invincible moral courage.

Courage he had to have throughout his career. It took courage for him even to join the Dominican Order. Like his celebrated pupil, Thomas Aquinas, he had a vocation that was objected to by his family, who hoped for a more worldly calling for the young heir of the house of Böllstadt than that of an impoverished priest. They were not so dramatic in their objections as the family of Aquino. They did not own the brisk Italian imagination. For the story goes that Thomas's relatives, hoping to break his will toward celibacy, insinuated one night into his cell a beautiful and naked girl instructed to seduce him from his vows; and that Thomas, waking to this vision of wantonness, thrust at her with "a lighted brand" so that she fled his room in terror; and that he was "never again assailed by demands of the flesh." Men of the cloth seemed to have liked direct action. The tale reminds one of Luther's midnight encounter with the Devil, when he routed the Fiend by flinging an inkpot at him.

Albert's relatives simply argued with their boy, assuring him (quite rightly) that joining the Dominicans would interfere with his material progress. It did. It also interfered with his secular avocation, for he was constantly being called on all his life to be an administrator or a bishop or the head of some college, when he ought to have been left alone to notice the habits of birds and beasts and the true nature of the world.

But in one way his profession as friar aided his studies. For he traveled over Europe, as a penniless monk should, on foot. The Continent gave him the nickname of "the Bishop of the Boots." And while he walked he watched everything about him. He was, as F. Sherwood Taylor has said in a speculative essay, "like so many Germans, indefatigable, of immense strength and vitality, and totally devoted to his work."

The work he accomplished might now seem elementary, but we must remember this was the first half of the thirteenth century when science was little more than alchemy or metaphysics. It was a small branch, only, of the wholesale philosophy then constituting the respectable and accredited knowledge of the time. The earth was expected to be apprehended by "the natural powers of the mind," by logic, mathematics, ethics, rather than by observation and experiment. Albert was an innovator who relied on the last two. But he stood only tiptoe at the door of genuine science. He never entered the real garden. Still, like his less amiable contemporary Roger Bacon, he kept the gate ajar so that a later Newton could walk freely through it.

And how industrious he was! His writings, which fill thirty-eight quarto volumes, comment on every subject conceivable to the mind of his epoch. He wrote about physics, geography, astronomy, mineralogy, and biology; he proved to his own and his pupils' satisfaction that the world was indeed round. Treatises on botany and animal physiology poured from his hand, and he was able to disprove certain fantasies handed down from the ancients such as Pliny—for instance that "eagles wrap their eggs in fox skins and leave them to hatch in the sun." He traced the chief mountain ranges of Europe, explained the influence of latitude on climate, and all the while was attempting the painful task of reconciling faith with reason.

And all this without benefit of telescope, microscope, test tubes, or any of the multitudinous tools without which scientists today could scarcely take a step. In his spare time he rewrote the works of Aristotle "to make them more acceptable to Christian critics," and it was on the foundation of his thought that Aquinas built his own palace of intellect.

Nor was this done without obstruction. The road of the pioneer is seldom easy. Besides being in demand as an administrator, he was also constantly having to defend his studies and their orthodoxy. His last public appearance was at Paris, where in old age he hurried to the university there to explain the theories of his dead pupil and darling, Aquinas, and to maintain that they in no way erred against established theology. He was not completely successful, for lesser men such as Stephen Tempier, Bishop of Paris, managed to get both master and pupil condemned on certain points. It took more than fifty years for the writings of either to be declared wholly acceptable to a reactionary clergy.

Science has its martyrs, as has religion. The most famous is Galileo, but in a way Albert falls into that category. He was never physically harmed—the Inquisition was in its fledgling stage and, even though it was the Dominicans who headed it, the order protected its own—but he was harassed to a certain extent, disappointed and impeded. Any age resents being reft of its hoarded superstitions. When one realizes that more than four centuries after Albert, Cotton Mather in supposedly enlightened New England was insisting on the actuality of witches and mermaids, it is easy to understand why the Universal Doctor made society in his day nervous with his obstinate demand for method and proof.

So suspect was he that even his canonization got delayed for hundreds of years. Although he achieved a laggard beatitude in 1622, it was not until 1931 that Pope Pius XI proclaimed him a Doctor of the Catholic Church and thus an authentic saint, patron of students. And, in truth, nothing about his busy life gives the same impression of transcendent holiness that we feel in his angelic protégé, Thomas. Nevertheless it is easy to give him our affection. His mighty effort was to bring science into tandem with philosophy. Today we reverse the process, trying to philosophize science. We need both disciplines. The closer they are connected the better for the world. Any thinking person realizes how barren is a planet deprived of an ethical base for its marvelous but mischievous inventions. I like to imagine that an Albert now would be turning to ecology, attempting to keep the nature he so loved in harmony with itself. And he would still be the good and learned Swabian, personification of Germanic talent at its apogee.

To run through a list of saints who typify their national characteristics would take a book the size of Albert's own. Except for the greatest of them they cannot help speaking to us and to God in a local dialect. But I cannot overlook the English. I could name a dozen who fulfill the qualifications of national genius. One could make out a good case for Thomas More, with his understated wit, his legalistic approach to martyrdom, the austerities which he kept secret even from his own family. Yet I have in mind a different sort of Englishness, one which is often overlooked in a survey of the British character but which runs like a luminous thread through the fabric of their history. It is the spirit of romantic adventure, the insouciance of a Drake, a Raleigh, a Lord Nelson—and not so long ago of the heroes of the RAF, flying their outnumbered planes so dashingly that they themselves have become legend.

Peril brings out this cavalier strain. And never at any time were conditions riper to evoke it than the reign of the first Elizabeth, when the Spanish threat on the secular side and the divisions of the Reformation on the other were both molding men of intense and whimsical courage. The fellow who best fits this debonair role is a young Jesuit named Edmund Campion, the most dashing holy man who ever played hounds and hare with fate. He is a kind of spiritual Scarlet Pimpernel, reckless, gallant, glorying at once in his mission and in outwitting his pursuers.

In order to savor his exploits we must understand what was then going on in prosperous but troubled England. The Roman Catholic Church, when it is being more Roman than catholic, has committed a number of political errors. One of the sorriest was the Bull issued by Pope Pius V, a good man but tactless. He could possibly have healed the breach between England and the Vatican that Henry VIII had initiated; instead, in a fit of self-righteous indignation, and quite misunderstanding the implacable patriotism of Englishmen, he chose to excommunicate Elizabeth and all her subjects who subscribed to the new Church. A schism already existed. By this edict it was turned into complete revolt. Elizabeth retaliated by wholly outlawing the old faith. Popish leanings must be wiped out in the island. Saying mass was made an illegal act.

Families who refused to follow the Book of Common Prayer or who did not attend the lawful Sunday services were either heavily fined or carried off to the Tower.

But laws, as everyone knows, cannot at once stamp out old loyalties. The Roman religion went underground but it continued. (Not even Cromwell was able completely to abolish it. It took the pragmatic nineteenth century to make England a truly Protestant kingdom.)

So Elizabeth's regime, already a militarily adventurous one, became domestically one of informers and midnight raids; of hunted priests being hidden for months in manors and farm houses; of masses said on the wing and heard in secret. After Campion came the famous "Priests' Holes," developed by that winning genius with carpenter's tools, Blessed Nicholas Owen. So cleverly did Nicholas construct his hideaways that even today they are being freshly discovered in old houses. Had Campion had the benefit of such an escape hatch, he might have survived longer than he did. For he was one of the first Jesuits sent from Douay into England, not to foment a civil rebellion (although the Pope would probably have winked at that) but to comfort still loyally Catholic families trying to resist apostasy.

The fittest adjective to apply to Campion, I think, is "Elizabethan." He was truly a man of his century, avid for learning, ambitious, filled with the spirit of the High Renaissance. He came of modest people. His father was a book seller in London. But his was the day when the new learning, the thrust of the Renaissance, filled the land with excitement. Wealthy citizens were everywhere rushing to endow schools and colleges; and not only the upper classes attended them. There were scholarships for promising boys. Campion, having at fifteen already attracted notice for his talents, was admitted to Oxford. There he did brilliantly even in an atmosphere of uniform brilliance. All the academic plums fell into his hands. He was made a junior fellow, acquired a reputation for oratory (a skill as important then as it had been in the time of

Demosthenes), and was chosen to make the speech of welcome to Elizabeth when she visited Oxford in 1566.

He so dazzled her and the royal retinue that they made a pet of him. Leicester gave him lordly favor and Cecil, then at the height of his glory, referred to him as "one of the diamonds of England." Everything prospered for him. Since he came from a soundly Protestant family, no impediment seemed to stand in the way of a great career— a bishopric, perhaps, affluence, government office.

And then he threw it all away. How or when he began to have qualms, to doubt the authenticity of the Church to which he was already attached as a deacon, the records do not tell. A watcher cannot understand all behavior patterns of his quarry; can only observe actions, not dissect the soul beneath the plumage. On the face of it Campion had seemed a perfectly contented creature of the Establishment. But Oxford, seething with intellectual ferment as all good universities do, had its own group of philosophical dissidents. The Thirty-Nine Articles had only recently been adopted as the new Creed. Probably scholars argued over these as ours now argue war and civil justice. The boy had a conscience, and it wakened. At any rate, Edmund, the young man on his way up the worldly ladder, turned by degrees into Campion the resister. He could no longer give his soul's allegiance to the Church of England.

But the most we know about his spiritual adventures is that he began to make his doubts audible. And that does appear to be in character. He could be a dissembler for love's sake but never for his own.

Presently England, apprehensive over any signs of recusancy in important quarters, became too hot for him and he left the country—left Oxford, his friends, all the rewards on which his youthful mind had been centered. As most of the fleeing Catholic intellectuals were doing then, he made his way to the University at Douay in Belgium. It was a sort of headquarters for the English, particularly; and it was also populous with Jesuits, who were reaping a harvest of novices. Campion was drawn to this stimulating group, took a degree, and joined the Society. That was common enough in a day when religious fervor was at a very high pitch, when men of conscience turned to holy orders as they now rush into political battles. What was uncommon was the rapidity with which Campion took over his mission as the first returning apostle to his countrymen.

I doubt that the authorities in Prague, where he had been sent to teach after being ordained in Rome, realized how dangerous that mission was. But Campion understood, and so did another English Jesuit, Robert Parsons, who was chosen as his companion. By what we know of them both, it was that very danger they rejoiced in. No paratrooper dropped behind the lines during World War II ever reveled more in playing a perilous game where the stakes were uncomplicated matters of life and death.

The two traveled, of course, in disguise. This was vital, for they had not only to reach the English ports, they had also to pass through the Protestant canton of Geneva, where Catholics were no more welcome than in London. In Geneva Campion pretended to be an Irish serving man called Patrick (he had recently returned from a brief mission to that green island) and "behaved," so Butler writes, "with that reckless cheerfulness that makes more serious-minded people think the English are mad." Having survived this challenge, they set out for England, "Parsons, disguised as a returning soldier from the Lowlands, followed by Campion as a jewel merchant, with his servant, a coadjutor-brother, Ralph Emerson." And somehow they made it across the Channel.

Peril was their constant company. There were spies everywhere, and Elizabeth's government soon learned the pair were in the country. Up started the hue and cry. Parsons' danger was real, but it was nothing compared to Campion's on account of his wide reputation. A monarch dares not forgive a favorite who has played her false. Parsons was only a nuisance. Edmund was a genuine threat, and all the hounds of the pursuivants were set upon his trail.

The whole adventure was absurdly Quixotic from start to finish. But it was extraordinary how long and how cunningly Campion managed to stave off arrest. Much of the credit goes, of course, to the brave men and women who sheltered him in attics and outhouses, in hidden rooms and concealed storage places, and always at the risk of their own lives. Still, he got on with the work he was sent to do. He made converts. He served mass in innumerable houses. He ranged from London to Berkshire, Oxfordshire, Lancashire, roving, hiding, preaching, again hiding. It no doubt tickled his romantic fancy to be constantly changing clothes and personalities—now the ruffed and doubleted country gentleman, now the loutish groom.

"I ride about some piece of the country every day," he wrote to the Father General of the Jesuits. "The harvest is wonderful great. . . . I am in apparel to myself very ridiculous; I often change it and my name also. I read letters sometimes myself that, in the first front, tell news that Campion is taken, which roused, in every place where I come so filleth my ears with the sound thereof that fear hath taken away all fear."

Even so industriously dodging about, he still managed to write a Latin treatise which was called *Decem Rationes,* in which he offered to dispute with learned Protestant ministers on matters of doctrine. His most celebrated literary effort, though, is a letter addressed to the Privy Council in the hope that if and when he was captured he might receive a fair trial. It has come down to us by the title of "Campion's Brag." It wasn't a boast, exactly; it rather spelled out his position as a good subject of the Queen and no traitor. But it did insist that on matters of religion he owned a moral right to say mass and teach the old faith.

Both publications took weeks to turn out on the simple printing presses of the era, worked on stealthily by volunteers. By Campion's standards they were free of sedition, but they were inflammatory to the explosive passions of a

fidgety realm ready to take fire. England was a far cry
from the tolerant nation which now permits any sort of
dissension so long as it does not cause a "public disturb-
ance." And anyhow, Campion was not a careful man but
a headstrong adventurer. *Decem Rationes* he caused to
be placed on church benches in Oxford to catch the attention of local scholars. He did not mean to issue his Brag
except in an emergency. But that latter cheerful document got prematurely distributed about the country by
mistake, and it was a sensation.

This outrageous Jesuit who seemed to be mocking his
pursuers had to be found. More men were sent after him,
more rewards offered. His advisers, amateurs like himself
but more prudent, tried to persuade Edmund he must go
to ground for a while. Had he been less valorous (or less
rash) he might have returned to the Continent until the
chase had dwindled. It was the course Father Parsons
finally took. The good Robert, not so important as Campion
to the Queen's agents, eventually escaped. He made his
way to Rouen, went on to Rome, and ended his life peacefully there as rector of the English College.

Campion, however, refused to budge. The most he consented to do was to take temporary refuge in the house
of a Mrs. Yates. And in her residence, while he was blithely
giving Communion to some forty neighbors, he was taken.
There had been a spy in the congregation.

The rest makes sad if gallant reading. There was, of
course, no hope for him. It was not simply that he had
broken laws; he had had the effrontery to break them
with *élan*. Now he himself had to be broken.

The Queen was cautious even if he was not. She and
her counselors did not desire a martyr; they knew how
well martyrdoms water the seeds of dissent. If they could
persuade this celebrated prize to apostasize, it would do
their cause far more good than hanging him. So while he
was in the Tower several powerful advocates were sent
to lead him up onto a mountain top and show him the
kingdoms of earth. The Earls of Bedford and Leicester

came with tempting offers of preferment would he only admit that Gloriana was legitimately head of the English Church. Elizabeth herself is said to have visited him. It was useless. Evidently the Kingdom of Heaven offered him a more charming prospect than all others.

So the torturers had their way with him. He was racked twice almost to death, and, while still too weak to raise his arms, was again confronted by scholarly clergymen brought in to dispute with him. He not only vanquished them; he managed from his bed to conduct his own defense. He also did a very saintly thing. It was a certain Mr. Eliot who had betrayed him. This gentleman now went in fear of his life, for the English have never loved a Judas. A good many people in the country were saying that Campion was innocent of any real crime. Eliot paid him a visit, perhaps from remorse, more likely out of fright. Campion not only forgave him; he also suggested the fellow should leave England and handed him a letter of recommendation to a German nobleman in whose house the betrayer might be safe. History does not tell us what happened to Eliot. But it does record Edmund's inevitable execution.

The barbarous custom at political hangings then was to disembowel the victim even before life had been extinguished. Some of Campion's blood is supposed to have splashed on a pair of young men, a poet named Henry Walpole and Philip Howard, Earl of Arundel. Both became converts and later themselves martyrs.

But that is a pietistic story, and I tell Campion's more in admiration for his Elizabethan swagger than because he joined the immense company of those who have died bravely for a cause. Martyrs are not unique. We have them even now. What endears him to me and has made him a particular patron of the order he helped glorify is that mad Englishness of his. He could have sprung from no other race.

Always, of course, remain the grand exceptions. In some saints nationality is burned away by magnificence. The whole earth claims them. Little Francis, in his youth so essentially an Assisian gallant, now belongs to everybody. We can no more chain him solely to his hill town than we can shape Teresa of Avila into the stereotype of a Spanish nun. Thomas of Aquino may have been resolutely Italian by heritage, yet he is as untrammeled by the fetters of a single province as the Greek Aristotle whom Aquinas spent his life attempting to Christianize.

Of all the beguiling company, perhaps Augustine of Hippo escapes most soaringly from his era and his race. He is not the serenest saint in the calendar, not the meekest or most holy. He is simply universal.

It is tempting to type-cast him as tempestuous Mediterranean, a man from North Africa whose Numidian blood warred with his Latin education to form a peculiar temperament. Especially now when it is the ambition of sociologists to prove how indebted we are to African culture and non-Aryan talents, we could find him useful as a weapon against racism. But black Africa has given us other saints and other intelligences to prove this necessary thesis. In fact, many of the great men of his time whom we take for granted as Europeans, such as Terence and Apuleius, were native Africans like him. We do not need him for a case history.

He is Everyman, exemplar of sensual humanity struggling to subdue his appetites and bend his intellect to the service of what he conceived of as righteousness. That he succeeded only partially is what has made him so enduring a figure to fifteen centuries of strivers—and of readers.

For, naturally, it is his *Confessions* that allow us to see him plain. Probably his is the greatest autobiography ever written. Since the year 399 it has enchanted all who encounter it, from atheists to theologians. In it lives a man as genuine as ourselves, a creature longing for harmony and order in his life but to whom nothing human was ever alien. God was the audience he ostensibly addressed, but frightened people of the late twentieth century hear him across the ages as if he existed now. Perhaps never since his age *until* now has he seemed more contemporary.

Confusion and violence were the marks of his era as they are of ours. He was born in 354, in Tagaste (currently the Algerian hamlet of Souk Ahras), a small city belonging to the decaying Carthaginian empire. Carthage had once shone as a beacon for the world. Washed by the Mediterranean, that sea which so richly nourished man's earliest gifts, it had a high culture that vied with Rome's. But power has its dangers. Rome looked to the south and noticed a rival.

"Cato and his sour like," writes Rebecca West, "held the mean man's myth that the prosperous man can only prosper at the expense of another man, and saw Carthage as the competitor of Rome, and provoked the Punic Wars. The victory of Rome in those wars left Carthage rubble and turned North Africa into a mere colony, where African men of genius were still born, but had to work without the support of their national tradition."

They had also to work without the support even of Rome itself, which was falling to pieces under the assaults of the barbarians. Chaos was Augustine's inheritance. Anarchy walked the streets, and no settled morality informed his time. His very rearing sounds familiar to the modern ear.

He came of a mixed marriage, his father a pagan landowner, his mother, Monica, a devout Christian. And he inhabited a world as materialistic as ours. Nothing seems more natural to us than his parents' determination to force on their clever son an education which would fit him for that material world and make him a financial success. There were no great corporations then, no law firms or scientific professions to make his fortune. But it was an epoch that still loved learning and philosophy, and the quickest route to renown was schoolmastering. Many a prominent man of the day had become famous by establishing an academy of rhetoric where scholars flocked to study and dispute. Since Augustine's father, Patricius, had other children, Augustine could expect little revenue from the family's small estates. The boy must depend on his education-sharpened wits.

So he was early set to work at Greek and Latin and mathematics. In his book he tells it all. He forgets nothing, and in a way forgives nothing. Despite the piety of his intent, he cannot quite cast out the resentments he held against the System. He confesses that he always hated Homer because of the beatings he received as a schoolboy trying to master Greek (Latin he got in infancy from his nurse). He is still angry at the elders who laughed at his punishments. One feels that a milder saint would have long ago forgiven these routine floggings, but not this passionate soul who hated injustices of any sort, even those committed against himself. Virgil still arouses his animosity. "I was forced to memorize the wanderings of Aeneas —whoever *he* was," he cries hotly, and we realize that, for all his trek toward virtue, rancor lives in him still.

But then he leaves out nothing of himself, good or bad, and the story retains an urgent immediacy. Indeed, the book's style could not be more in vogue than it is now. The baring of one's psyche and one's sins in confessional poetry or prose sustains the mass of today's best sellers. There is, however, one enormous difference. Augustine is not boasting or attempting to titillate the reader. He never shows off, only instructs; accuses but does not whine. "This is what it is like," he tells us, "to be a human being in search of his soul." And in doing this he enlarges the limits of our human knowledge. No one has ever better understood man's mind, man's temptations, man's motives.

Everything is set down with perfect honesty. (He even tries, long before Freud, to get at the roots of infant behavior.) There is the child who shirked his lessons. There are his academic successes in Carthage, where he went to study at seventeen and plunged first into the sensuality which plagued him so long. He tells us about the beginning of his affair with the mistress who bore him his adored son, Adeodatus. We listen also to the innumerable voices of those oracles who were the seducers of his age as they are of ours, everywhere whispering—or shouting—doom and prophecies of escape from that doom. Particularly there is his early quest for the meaning of existence which led to his involvement with the then popular cult of the Manichees. It is characteristic of Augustine, the lover of literature, that he was drawn to his mother's Christianity but turned away from it chiefly because its sponsors and its writings were not sufficiently graceful to suit his fastidious taste.

We see him setting up his schools of rhetoric, first at Tagaste, then at Carthage, and of his tribulations with students as unruly as university protesters today. He says his classes were interrupted by "the riotous incursions of blackguardly youngsters." While they may have burned no professorial papers or kidnaped no deans, they were so pestilential that the young scholar in disgust left Africa for Rome. Student manners were better in that city, but he had difficulty collecting his fees and finally settled with his mistress and his son in Milan, where his reputation as an outstanding teacher notably improved. So did his finances.

But by this time God was at his heels. Even while he was plunging deeper into frivolity and lust, he was agonizingly trying to believe in a spiritual existence. Manichaeism, with its fantasy realms of pure evil and pure good, no longer satisfied him. Beyond everything else, Augustine was logical. His mind had to feed on facts, and Christianity appeared to him factual as well as exalted. He began to attend the lectures of Saint Ambrose, revered in Milan as much for his scholarship as for his religious message. They met and the friendship flourished. Augustine admits he was drawn to the older man for secular reasons; it was learning that attracted him more than the Christ Ambrose preached. Still, the Gospels lured him. He had tried vice and it offered him no peace. He longed to be delivered from depravity—from sloth and greed and irregular sexual behavior and all those sins which have eternally exhausted the resources of heaven-aspiring men.

Like the rest of us, though, he kept putting off the decision to reform. To the God he was starting to trust, he incessantly repeated (he writes) nothing except "drowsy words, 'presently, by and by, let me alone a little longer.'"

Monica, her husband dead, had followed her brilliant but difficult son to Milan. While she was with him she accomplished something rather strange and not very generous by our standards. Seeing his inward restlessness, she persuaded Augustine that marriage was exactly the thing to settle him. He must put away his mistress and become a husband. (The one thing we do not learn from his *Confessions* is why he never considered making a wife out of his son's mother.) A marriage was arranged with a supposedly suitable girl and his long-time love went back to Tagaste, swearing she would "never know another man." My heart goes out to this unknown woman, so faithful, so magnanimous that she left behind with his father their one dual possession, Adeodatus. And here is where Monica, saint though she is proclaimed, seems so short-sighted. Augustine's fiancée may have been correct as to status and dowry; but she was still too young to marry. The suitor would have to wait two years for the ceremony.

How could Monica have believed he was ready to live like a monk for twenty-four months? By losing his mistress, he says, his "heart was broken and wounded and shed blood . . . but I was unable to bear the delay of two years which must pass before I was to get the girl I had asked for in marriage. In fact, it was not really marriage that I wanted. I was simply a slave to lust. So I took another woman . . . and thus was my soul's disease nourished and kept alive as vigorously as ever."

To this generation's free-minded youth, what he thought of as his great sin would not sound very terrible. But every age has its moral goals. Social justice is one of our slogans. The fourth century idealized chastity—perhaps because it was so rare. And even in his dissipations, Augustine could not shrug off concern for something in life larger than his own desires. He and several friends used to meet to discuss philosophy and religion, even at one time planned to band together into a small community dedicated to the "peace we hoped to attain." The plan came to nothing, but the discussions continued. He read Plato—in a Latin translation, since he still hated Greek. He read Paul's Epistles. He ached to become a Christian, but bodily delights and the fear he would have to give them up came between him and baptism.

"Soon," he went on murmuring to God. "Just give me a little time." Like the rest of mankind he hoped an impossible hope, that his will would not have to be exerted, that temptations would by some miracle cease to vex him and his bad habits simply roll off his shoulders by themselves.

Then came the famous moment in the garden "under a fig tree" when he heard a child's voice chanting the refrain, "Take up and read, take up and read." He had on a table beside him "the Apostle's Book" and on opening it he read the passage "upon which my eyes first fell: 'Not in rioting and drunkenness, not in chambering and impurities, not in contention and envy, but put ye on the Lord Jesus Christ and make not provision for the flesh in its concupiscences.'"

The pilgrim had his sign, his light on the road to a personal Damascus.

He was only thirty-two, but the way was set. There were to be many wrestlings thereafter but no crises. The rest of his life, full of works and deeds and books and disputations as it was, flowed steadily forward along the path that yearning had laid out for him. Actually he traveled a road which sanctity has made familiar. First he withdrew from the city with a few friends and converts to a country retreat for prayer and austere practices, a monastic community where "all things were in common and were distributed according to everyone's needs." That apprenticeship done, he returned to Africa as apostle to his native province. Griefs did not forsake him. First Monica died, than Adeodatus. But the waverings were over. He had not planned to be a priest, but in those harried days any outstanding Christian scholar was likely to be drafted into some clerical seat; and he found himself presently head of the Bishopric of Hippo, where he was to work and rule for nearly forty years. And all the while he tried with every fiber of his soul for holiness and temperance, for meekness and charity—and succeeded very well, considering the incorrigibly human material he had to work with. For, although he was certainly devout, always affectionate and friendly "even toward infidels," and indubitably a genius, the fire of nature refused to quit him. He remained to the day of his death Everyman, given to rages and depressions, quick in argument and intolerant of opposition.

He came into conflict with Jerome and emerged second best from the claws of that old lion. Having been converted from Manichaeism, he turned the full force of his polemics on that sect and helped demolish its influence. He proved kind Pelagius a heretic. He founded a school of theology which has informed Western thought for all these centuries, both expanding and harming it, for his was the dour doctrine of predestination, a dogma we find ungracious today. It took a genius as universal as he to give us a gentler way of thinking, an Aquinas who made peace between Augustine harshness and Aristotle's concept of a merciful Shaper.

But for all his human flaws, this extraordinary man possessed one virtue that makes him a true saint. That single quality has permitted him to live undaunted in Christian annals as well as in secular and contemporary letters. The quality was that which, most of any, we need today—the virtue of hope.

If we find ourselves despairing now, think how much more reason he had then to call things into question. By 413 his world, so long toppling, was at the brink of dissolution. Alaric had already plundered Rome. The Vandals were preparing to invade North Africa. Augustine's civilization was not only imperiled; it was doomed. Yet while the city of man was falling, he sat down and wrote the book which, next to the *Confessions*, is his greatest work. It was *The City of God*, and on its premises the Western World, once it had recovered a little from the shock of its wounds, began to build itself once more. This superb tract was finished in 426, just about the time Saint Patrick was making his way to Ireland with both faith and literature in his saddlebags, where in the amber of uninvaded tranquillity they were to be preserved until Europe was ready to take them back.

Hope implies courage, and that Augustine had in abundance. Have I called him Everyman? I mean it in its sublimest sense: Everyman assailed by all the sorrows and seductions of the world but overcoming them, realizing by his fierce efforts the highest potentials of the human spirit.

He died as he had lived, still uncrushed by the troubles that weighed upon him. The Vandals under Gaiseric had overrun North Africa, were actually besieging Hippo when Augustine was "seized by a fever" to which he succumbed. He had lasted long enough to see most of his work seemingly undone, the churches in ruins, the cities razed. But even in defeat he gave over his will to the Ultimate. "I ask God to deliver this city from its enemies," he prayed, "or if that may not be, that He give us strength to bear His will."

He had come a great way from the thirty-year-old rebel who had fled so persistently from the Hound of Heaven.

His writings survived even if his city did not. And no man ever did more to revivify civilization when it began to crawl out of the ruins and lift its battered head.

His birthplace was Africa. But the place where he forever rests is in the world's heart.

The Spaniard

His life was a paradox.

To begin with, he was not Spanish at all but a Basque.
Yet no more typically Spanish saint ever tilted a lance
against an enemy.

A hidalgo, a caballero, a small-statured gentleman from
the province of Navarre, Ignatius Loyola, founder of the
Jesuits, wears the other face of Cervantes' hero. He is
Don Quixote, but a successful Don, one whose windmills
turned out to be real foes he was able to vanquish, whose
Dulcinea existed and was beautiful.

Every facet of what we think of as the Spanish character
belonged to him. He was proud to excess. He was romantic, valorous, jealous of personal dignity. He owned to
an exorbitant degree a sense of honor and a thirst for adventure which even in his last busy years, fettered as he
was then to a strict administrative desk, never deserted
him. The latter quality he simply passed on to his sons in
the Order and sent them roaming about the world in search
of glory. It was, of course, a different sort of glory from
that which he planned in his swaggering youth.

To be a soldier of Spain, to win celebrated battles and
the love of some highborn lady, was the dream that con-
sumed him for the first thirty-odd years of his life. He
seemed so little made of the stuff of sanctity that he is

almost a case history of converted man. Unlike the young Augustine, he seems never to have done any wrestling with his soul. He was content to act out his inherited role as brawler and dueler and señor-about-town. He strutted the streets of Castilian cities like a gamecock, fastidious in his dress if not his morals, careful that his auburn hair was well combed and his hands cared for, and ready to draw a sword if any other dandy so much as jostled him in passing.

His posture was a natural one, for he came of a haughty and cantankerous family. His home was the little Castle of Loyola near Azpeitia in Guipúzcoa, and he was son and grandson of soldiers. In fact, his grandfather had been so inclined to challenge his neighbors, on any pretext, to a feudal combat that the King of Castile had been forced to demilitarize the castle and forbid that old knight the rights of private warfare. By the time Ignatius was born in 1491 the fortunes of the house had a bit declined. But its youngest cadet (the last of thirteen children) grew up with a firm determination to increase them by his prowess at arms.

It was a time of harvest for such ambitions. Columbus had discovered America, Spain was extending her empire, the long struggle with the Moslems was ending, and riches glittered in the Iberian air. Any mettlesome gentleman could make his fortune either by soldiering or on foreign expeditions.

We do not know much about the saint's childhood. He was sent to learn something called "the exercises of a gentleman" at the court of Queen Isabella's chief treasurer, but the rest of his early education must have been rudimentary and anything but classical. It is characteristic of his nature and training that we first hear of him in authentic history as a culprit haled before the judges in Guipúzcoa for a street quarrel. In the documents of that affair we even have a word portrait of how he then looked and behaved.

He wore "long locks down to his shoulders, and parti-colored hose and a colored cap. And," the report goes on, "he usually appeared in public in a leather cuirass and breastplate, carrying sword, dagger, musket, and all other sorts and descriptions of weapons." He is also recorded as being of an amorous bent (*"satis liber in mulierum amore"*). In other words, he was a typical Spanish gallant of his era and his station.

"It was the bad way of his world," writes James Brodrick, his wittiest and best biographer, "and he had, at any rate, the reputation of being a chivalrous and very generous foe who bore no malice against his enemies and always fought like a gentleman."

It was fighting in battle on a disadvantaged side that altered the course of his aspirations.

Defending the garrison at Pamplona against an overwhelming regiment of French invaders, he was wounded in both legs by a cannon ball. The chivalrous French, recognizing in him an enemy worthy of regard, did what they could for his injuries and sent him back to Loyola on a litter. At home again, the young captain found he could expect no rapid recovery. That cherished right leg which had gone so jauntily stockinged had to be broken again and reset. There began for Ignatius what even he, who despised complaining, later referred to as "that butchery." His Spanish doctors seem to have been no cleverer than the French. The left leg healed but on the right one, bone still protruded below the knee. So the first operation was followed by another, and that was followed by a session with a rack, a sort of primitive traction designed to pull the fracture back into place so both legs might eventually be again the same length. Considering that this was long before the age of anesthetics, the whole process seems to us an ordeal almost beyond human strength. But Ignatius endured it in stoic—and Spanish—silence. If he was to win fame as a soldier, he must walk again no matter what the cost in brutal pain.

After a gangrenous infection, from which for a while he was not expected to rally, he spent months in bed, immobilized and miserable. While he waited out the time until he could move about once more, he began to read. Reading is the invalid's diversion, and Ignatius thought it might be a handsome way of passing his difficult days if he could lose himself in tales of romantic adventure, of knights at their exploits, and fair ladies being rescued from peril. The Loyola household, however, did not own much of a library. The only books at hand, dusty and unread, were the preposterous stories of Amadis de Gaul and a few devotional works such as the *Flowers of the Saints.*

Well, a book is a book. Ignatius read what the family brought to his bedside and at length found himself particularly enjoying the more pious of the sagas. After all, they were peopled by heroes who endured in the face of danger, who fought battles of the soul and achieved celestial victories. (They were also no doubt heavily embroidered with legend.) Ever a romantic, the ruined soldier found his imagination catching fire of a new sort. Perhaps there were higher roles a man might play on earth than that of warrior. Remember, he was weakened and susceptible. Remember also that this was an age when to be a loyal Spanish gentleman meant to be a Christian and a Catholic. For all his cockerel lustiness, he had never been a cynic about religion. He had merely never given it much thought. If he had to go limping all his days, if he was to be thwarted in worldly matters, why not, he wondered, enlist in another sort of regiment? It was little more than emulation that inflamed him first. He was enchanted by difficulties, by the notion of being heroic. What other men had done he, a Loyola, could do also.

The experience of Ignatius is a rebuttal to the easy, often-repeated sophistry that "nobody was ever seduced by a book." Since the invention of writing, books have seduced men's minds and souls, have turned them toward good or evil, vice or honor, revolution, reaction, patriotism, treason, atheism, or religion. Paul's Epistle seduced Augustine. Thomas Paine's tracts helped make the French Revolution. A potboiler called *Uncle Tom's Cabin* was one of the fuses that lit the Civil War. Books are the most puissant weapons on earth, and we, in this word-ridden age, ought to give thought to their power. For we not only become what we imitate; we also become what we read about and admire. Had Ignatius not been entranced by what may have been little more than trumpery legends, we would probably never have heard of him even as a footnote in history.

But those books begot ambition. He began to pray a good deal, to feel remorse for his past wanderings, and to look forward to following the grand pattern of his new heroes. "When I am walking again," he told himself, "I will go on pilgrimage to the Holy Land. I will be austere, sober, penitential—and maybe a great man."

He admitted in after years that he then understood nothing whatever of the virtues the saints he wished to follow had to exercise—humility, charity, patience, discretion. It was the outward work he saw, another version of the knight-errantry that had always beckoned him. Still, in even so small a way, he had released within himself a force, that touch of beatific genius, forever latent in the careless cavalier. Otherwise the new dream would have vanished when his invalidism ended.

But once on his feet, with only a slight limp remaining (which he would carry to the grave), he found his resolve still strong. He broke the news to his family that he was renouncing his military career for that of mendicant. They were not happy about his decision, but only a brother, Martin, tried hard to dissuade him. Perhaps the others felt it was a whim which would not last long; many a Spaniard had gone on pilgrimage before and returned to take up his old pursuits. Ignatius got around the pleas of his brother by telling him, quite truthfully, that he intended to go to Najera to rejoin the viceroy, who had recently offered him a splendid commission. As a man of his word he did travel first to Najera. But he stayed only long enough to collect his accumulated back pay and settle a few debts, then rode off alone on a mule to the sanctuary of Montserrat in Catalonia.

On the road to Montserrat something happened which tells much about Ignatius and how far away he was from sanctity. Along the way he met a Moor, evidently a sociable and agreeable chap. But he was an infidel, and the orthodox Spaniard felt he ought to have a go at converting him. So badly versed was Ignatius in theology that the only topic he could think to argue was the virginity of Mary. "And what, sir, do you admit of that doctrine?" he asked fiercely. The polite Moslem had probably never given the matter a moment's thought, but he answered amiably enough that yes, he could concede Mary might well have been a virgin before the birth of her Son, but he did not quite see how she could have been afterward. It must have been a real concession for a non-Christian and made only out of civility. Yet after the pair had gone their separate ways Ignatius started brooding on the lack of conviction he sensed in the man's replies. He had met his first infidel and done nothing to change his faith. Was it not his duty to wipe the fellow and his heresies off the face of Spanish earth? A ridiculous dilemma? Certainly. The beginning of the Ignatian journey was all ridiculous viewed in the light of secular and twentieth-century opinion. He was then Don Quixote at his most comic.

After much inward debate, Ignatius decided to use a gambler's method of choice. If his mule turned toward the side road the Moor had taken, he would go after the blasphemer and stab him, although, naturally, in a fair fight. Otherwise he would leave him alone. Fortunately the animal sauntered on down the highway and Ignatius was saved from so absurd and terrible a deed.

One wonders what the fathers at the shrine of Montserrat would have given him as penance had he confessed to killing a perfectly inoffensive traveler. Perhaps they might have closed their ears from sheer fatigue. For Ignatius spent three days writing down all the sins he could re-

member from his past life before making there his general
confession. Once that duty was over, he gave away his
fashionable clothes to a tramp, hung up his arsenal, and
put on the garments of a pilgrim. These he had bought
earlier, and they consisted of exactly what the books had
told him the well-dressed man on his way to Jerusalem
ought to wear—sackcloth, sandals, a rope belt, and a con-
tainer for carrying water; also the correct pilgrim's staff.
His food he planned to beg along the wayside.

Naïvely he believed that nothing now stood between
him and the Holy Land. Like the knight he had not
ceased to be, he gave an extra flourish to the beginning
of his journey by keeping a twelve-hour vigil before the
altar of Our Lady, as one of the protagonists of old romances would have done before he set out to slay a
dragon. The next morning, refreshed in spirit if not in
body, he took the road for Barcelona, where he hoped
to find a ship. Passing through the town of Manresa, he
was delayed. It was a long delay and one that altered him
forever; altered also the shape of much of the world. For
he discovered he had to have Rome's permission for
transport to Jerusalem, and that was slow in coming. An
uneasy peace had settled on the Moslem-Christian earth
and a sensible Pope did not wish hordes of European travelers debouching upon the sacred shrines in such numbers as to disturb the truce. While Ignatius waited, a
plague ravaged Barcelona and no one was allowed in or
out of that city. Manresa it would have to be for the impatient pilgrim. And Manresa it was for ten strange months.

The town became his wilderness, his desert, the place
where his rash soul endured its dark night and came forth
changed beyond recognition, tempered in God knows what
furnaces of suffering and despair. There, like other mystics,
he came into contact with what William James has named
the "supreme reality."

Psychologists might explain away his visions as deriving
from malnutrition and hysteria, and undoubtedly for those
ten months he was underfed and running a spiritual fever.

He lived on alms of the scantiest sort, allowing himself to beg only bread and water, with a "little wine to cheer him on Sundays if anyone offered it." He sheltered sometimes in a cave, sometimes in a hospice for the poor; now and then he was persuaded to sleep in a cell set aside for him by the Dominicans, who worried, with reason, about this extravagant penitent. For, true to romantic form, he tried at one wild extended session to invert all his former habits, as if overnight he could become another Anthony of Egypt. Had he, before, been fastidious about his person to the point of foppishness? Then he would let his hair and nails grow like an early hermit so that he might humiliate himself. He would sleep only two or three hours a day, fast every other week, pray until his knees were sore. Those old books had told him such austerities were the way of holiness, and he believed the printed word.

It was mad action, of course. And no doubt he *was* a little mad at times, as geniuses often are when they are committing works of art. During that decade of months he suffered such scruples, such hopelessness that he once considered flinging himself out of the nearest window. But there was steel in him as well as lunatic fervor. The amazing thing is not only that he did survive but that he emerged so rapidly from his desperation, famished but intact, with the fever gone and in his mind an entirely new concept of his mission and of himself. In that brief interlude his character had undergone miraculous changes. He who had been so foolish was beginning to be wise. Impetuosity had become prudence. The bigoted Spaniard, willing to assassinate an infidel for the honor of the Church, was filled with compassion and tolerance. (Later he was to teach his Jesuits that in arguing religion with anyone, no matter whether it was Protestant or pagan, any sort of recrimination was banned. Gentleness and politeness were to be their only weapons of debate.)

He was still a romantic, but now a brilliant sanity flooded his entire nature and he recognized his scruples for the neurotic symptoms they represented. He had also discovered what was to be his life's work—not anchoritic passivity but a positive apostleship. He was meant not to be an Anthony but a Paul.

As a first practical measure toward pulling himself together into military fitness, he cut his nails and hair and began to eat again, to sleep a sensible number of hours, and to put prayer itself into its proper perspective, as a luxury to be enjoyed at seemly times rather than in incessant occupation.

One seldom thinks of Ignatius as a profound intellect. That error probably arises from the fact that he was not literary. Only an intellect of the highest order could have transformed, and so quickly, the impulsive knight into the man of intense but sensible affairs. He was never a reformer, as many saints have been, attempting to rid the Church of its evils and weaknesses. (He did do that, but it was by example rather than polemics.) His was at once a narrower and more ambitious goal. Quite simply he wanted to convert the world.

He had brought out of his Manresan wilderness a tool with which he felt he might at least begin such an undertaking. It was the rough draft of his famous "Spiritual Exercises," on which the framework of Jesuit discipline is based.

Others of his kind, such as Teresa, Francis, John of the Cross, have returned from the nearly ineffable regions where Ignatius traveled with descriptive masterpieces. Francis wrote his *Canticles*, Teresa *The Interior Castle*, and John the verse that has endeared him to generations of literati. Ignatius came back from those realms not with a poem but a road map. If the others were the Ovids and Catulluses of mysticism he was the Caesar, jotting down his Commentaries. He had eloquence but it was always terse and soldierly.

At first the Exercises were designed only as an aid to himself and any floundering Christian he might encounter. Over many years he reworked and rewrote them until they became recognized as one of the most effective manuals of devotion ever composed, able to focus man's attention on the harmony of self-will with the will of God. They are a unique production, practical as a soldier's drill but filled with deep psychological perception, an almost hypnotic force of thought, and so celebrated have they grown that they have attracted intelligences so diverse as John Wesley's and Somerset Maugham's. (I must add that Maugham found them dry and unaffecting, which they must certainly seem to an agnostic. There is about them no touch of yoga, nothing to appeal to the vague aspirant or the skeptic.)

They are not even highly original except in form. Unlike Aquinas, Ignatius made no attempt to prove the existence of God. He was, as Christopher Hollis, the biographer, has said, "not a man of any deep historical learning or indeed at that stage of his life of any historical knowledge at all." He took it for granted that all ordinary men *knew* God existed, and had only to be led out of apathy and lethargy to follow His truths. Moreover, as a provincial Spaniard, he had scarcely felt the buffets of the Reformation; he seems hardly to have known at this time that Luther existed, although the two men were almost contemporaries. So he believed that he had only to point out to fellow Christians or to pagans how necessary it was to improve the state of their souls and they would find through his personal method the same beatitude he had discovered in Manresa.

With the notes in his pilgrim's bag, his health restored, and Barcelona once more accessible, he set off for the Holy Land, which was still the first port of call on his planned itinerary.

If he was looking for hardships he found them in plenty. He begged his way but would accept no more from charitable citizens than enough for a little food; anything left over he gave to the poor. A kind Barcelonian captain granted him free passage to Italy. Ignatius discovered that country itself now undergoing the plague, walked half its length to Venice, got permission from the doge for transport on a government ship to Cyprus, and after six months reached Jerusalem.

There for two ecstatic weeks he visited all the shrines and traced every sacred trail. Unfortunately the Don Quixote in Ignatius had not been entirely vanquished, and he was so filled with happiness and enthusiasm that he got the ill-advised notion of trying to convert some of Jerusalem's native population. The Franciscans, who were the authorized guardians of Christian places, politely but firmly suggested not only that he leave the inhabitants alone but that he also leave the country. It was his first defeat at the hands of a hierarchy, but far from his last. Still, he took it as he did others, with good grace; he found a ship on which to return to Europe and after a long journey home, during which he was usually wet, hungry, seasick, once within an inch of being arrested as a spy and within another inch of capture by the French, he made it back to Barcelona.

There he set to work on the next step of his program. Conscience and zeal alone had been enough for his own conversion. He did not think those qualities sufficient for his mission. If he was to work at bringing souls to Paradise he ought to be better educated in philosophy and theology than he now was. "I am a very ignorant man," he told a friend. "It is my punishment that I must go back to school."

So this gaunt, limping mendicant, already well over thirty and therefore middle-aged by the standards of his century, put himself, as it were, in kindergarten with children to acquire the Latin necessary for any sort of degree. He sustained his body on begged bread and his mind on the dry bones of grammar for two years. He then felt confident enough to enroll at the University of Alcalá. He still wore his pilgrim's dress and continued to give every spare moment to the instruction of penitents and to working and reworking the Spiritual Exercises, which he urged on everyone who would listen to him. It was not an auspicious time for such an enterprise. The Reformation was in full swing and those portions of Europe still orthodox grew nervous every time a new or unauthorized religious movement so much as raised a feeble head.

From Madrid came several inquisitors to investigate the case, and Ignatius found himself in prison off and on for months. Although the savants could discover nothing heretical about his preaching, they did suspect his enthusiasm. He was ordered to stop going about barefoot, to wear the clothes of an ordinary scholar instead of his sackcloth habit, and to leave off all religious instruction for three years. The latter blow was so bitter that he left Alcala for the famous university at Salamanca, hoping that in the anonymity of a city he might be left alone. He fared no better there, for again he ended in jail and was strictly forbidden his beloved project of "helping souls and directing his studies to that end."

The remark explains a good deal about Ignatius. Yes, he was an intellectual. But learning for its own sake did not mean very much to him. He was no fonder of Latin than Augustine had been of Greek. Jerome's passion for the pagan writers never afflicted him. His studies were strictly utilitarian, and the degree they would earn him only a passport to an apostleship of which the Church would not be suspicious.

So if Salamanca repudiated him he would leave the country entirely. Paris it must be, since the heavy arm of the Inquisition had not been able yet to throttle freedom at the colleges there. The fact that France and Spain, as usual, were at war and that he, as an enemy alien, would have trouble getting through combat lines and over hostile borders did not in the least daunt him. Driving a little donkey to carry his few books and armed with a letter of credit for twenty-five gold crowns collected for him by his friends in Barcelona, he set out on foot for the French capital. The money was meant to keep him alive while he studied, for he had learned—he was always, except for Latin grammar, a quick learner—that having to beg food and lodging interfered with the educational process. But a thief stole his money, the college of Montaigu, which he joined because there he could still study with children, was a harsh and terrible place, and he had to miss a number of evening lectures because the poorhouse where he was forced to live had an early curfew.

He looked for work, but no one wished to employ a limping Spaniard who did not even speak fluent French. Finally he took a term off to hurry into Flanders, renowned for its rich merchants with open purses. He went even to England, where, he says, he "collected such a store of alms" that he was able to eat again and to help other poor scholars. Ignatius hated to handle money—he embraced poverty as other men long for wealth—but he was becoming a practical man and recognized not only that funds for himself meant help for the poor of the city but that a bit of financial aid for his classmates drew them into his benign circle.

He also had the wisdom to leave Montaigu for the more humane college of Sainte Barbe "to brave," as Brodrick remarks, "for a second time the frowns of Aristotle."

The history of the next studious years in Paris differed little from the pattern of his first experiences there. He drank in great drafts of logic, philosophy, mathematics, theology—whatever the college had to offer—and adorned his mind without altering its steadfast purpose. For he spent nearly every hour he was not at his books preaching, counseling, explaining to those who were interested the worth of the Exercises. He drew about him a number of young men at the university, to whom he was both adviser and bursar, sharing his money when he had it, trotting off to accumulate a few guilders for them when the bank ran low. But he did finally graduate, and with honors. At the age of forty-three in 1534 he could write himself securely a master of arts of Paris.

From then on, with a certificate to prove his clerical credentials, he felt free to go on with his real apostleship, no longer merely at the college but to men and women

everywhere. Moreover, he was not alone. Even before his
graduation he had won six companions for his mission.
The most famous was Francis Xavier, a Basque like himself, but one whose family had fought on the other side of
the battle when Ignatius was wounded at Pamplona.

How the saint ever settled on Francis as a likely disciple is a mystery. That young gentleman, impoverished but
proud, was, at the start, contemptuous of everything for
which Ignatius stood. In fact, although he accepted aid,
he was rather ashamed of his shabby countryman. He,
Francis, was young and strong, an athlete, advanced in
Latin and winning prizes at the university. His future
seemed assured, and it certainly did not include a religious
vocation, particularly one inspired by this elderly cripple
who had already incurred the enmity of the Inquisition.
Perhaps Ignatius saw in this sprig of Navarrean nobility the
same ill-directed desires possessed once by himself; sensed
also the deep wells of feeling still untapped in him. At any
rate, he pursued Francis quietly and persistently for three
years until suddenly the skittish gallant gave way and
joined Ignatius to become, before he was through with
life, the most zealous, the most generous, and the
most world-beloved of the long procession of Jesuit saints.

The other five companions were Peter Fabre, so tender-
hearted he always included impartially in his prayers Martin Luther and the Pope; Diego Laynez, who was to be
general of the order after Ignatius's death, and Alfonso
Salmerson, Spaniards both, who had been taken under
the Loyolan wing when they arrived at Paris "without
enough French to order their dinners"; Nicholas Alfonso,
usually called Bobadilla, whose brusque manners and
fondness for the rich and distinguished gave the company
much amusement; and a Portuguese named Simon Rodriguez, who remained forever dear to Ignatius but a
constant thorn in his flesh for his moodiness and will-o'-the-
wisp character.

The seven decided to form themselves into a comradeship. They did not propose to live together in community

but would bind themselves to vows of poverty and chastity and gather frequently for discussion and "little festive meals." They would continue to study theology and at the same time direct their energies to deeds of charity and to moral teaching. In so quiet a fashion was founded the Society of Jesus, that group which ever since has drawn upon itself both the praise and obloquy of the world. It has, indeed, suffered from both in every century and every nation. No order (although it was not then yet an order) has had so controversial a history. Ignatius certainly could not foresee, on that pleasant Sunday in the country when the seven heard mass and swore their simple vows, that this company would one day sway kingdoms, help shoulder the Counter-Reformation, stem the tide of Protestantism in Europe, fly like birds to all four quarters of the globe on their tremendous missionary activities, rule a theological model state in Paraguay, institute a series of schools and universities over the world, split France (during the Port Royal squabble) into warring camps so that the country was almost lost to Rome's influence, and finally be suppressed, as they were for nearly half a century, by the very Pope whose elected army they were.

It is a curious thing, too, that Jesuits, designed for orthodoxy, should live their entire existence with the suspicion of heresy from other clergy; and that non-Catholics should admire them (or fear them) as fiercely as did their own denomination. Recently in an interview Reinhold Niebuhr admitted to having "an extravagant appreciation of the Jesuits" and pointed out that his "pro-Catholic moments are . . . chiefly pro-Jesuit moments."

Even those unaffectionate toward religion are moved by the circumstances of their founding. "Who is there," writes Balzac, "that would not admire the extraordinary spectacle of this union of seven men animated by a noble purpose who turn toward heaven and under the roof of a chapel lay down their worldly wishes and hopes and consecrate themselves to the happiness of their fellow men? They offer themselves as a sacrifice to the work of charity that shall give them no property or power or pleasure; they renounce the present for the future, looking forward only to a hereafter . . . and content with no happiness on earth beyond what a pure conscience can bestow."

Balzac evidently did not understand spiritual joyousness, for the seven, poor and unimportant, were probably the happiest fellows in France. Ignatius was never a jolly man—he was too Spanish for that—but he was always cheerful, and never so cheerful as in adversity. Francis was high-hearted as a lark, Peter Fabre overflowed with love for everything and everybody in sight, and even Bobadilla had a certain heavy humor. On one of their many journeys through lands at war and in the dead of winter, when they ate berries part of the time for sustenance and waded in mud and snow up to their thighs, Rodriguez reports that "so happy were they that their feet seemed not to be touching the ground at all."

They had what they wanted—a chosen poverty, their degrees as masters of arts, the hardships they aspired to, and the whole world to proselytize.

They first called themselves the Ignatians, sometimes the Pilgrims, and their only common project beyond acts of charity was an intense desire to get to Jerusalem, of whose delights Ignatius had told them. For two years they traveled about Europe, working in hospitals, teaching children or the ignorant, making friends and urging those friends toward the Exercises. Ignatius even went back for a while to Loyola, where, although the family had prepared to welcome him with feasts and comforts, so literally did he interpret his vow of poverty that he refused to stay anywhere except in a hospice and spent his time instructing the children of Guipúzcoa and preaching to curious if affectionate crowds. He also arranged for the relief of the region's poor people. Poverty he admired only for himself. He knew how hard was the beggar's role, and so set up a kind of Social Security scheme there, which he persuaded his family and wealthy families of the neighborhood to guarantee.

Then he joined his companions, increased in strength now to ten, in Venice, from which city they hoped to set sail to the Holy Land. While they waited for a ship, they once more took over the hard labor in hospitals. "We tend the patients," wrote Rodriguez, "make the beds, sweep the floors, scrub the dirt, wash the pots, dig the graves, carry the coffins, read the services, and bury the dead." He also adds that they were often themselves as weak as the patients with hunger and fatigue.

No ship ever sailed for them. The Turks and Venetians were at war and the ten made up their minds they must abandon their darling promise and turn to the alternative they had allowed themselves, that of going to Rome to offer their services to the Pope. So Rome it was, after, as usual, all sorts of mishaps and adventures along the route. The shape of their lives was coming clear to them. Ignatius had been, after Manresa, a guided missile, triggered and pointed in the right direction, but with the destination unclear. Now he knew his goal. If the Pope consented, they would turn themselves into an order and add two more vows to the ones they had already taken—obedience to a superior and a willingness to take up any mission on which Rome might send them.

They also agreed that, unlike the Benedictines and Franciscans, they should not be a strictly contemplative order. They would say their daily office privately and for meditation would lean on the Exercises. This was not for lack of ardor but because Ignatius, always an activist, wished to lop off from their duties any time-consuming rituals. And he demanded that they would as individuals accept no clerical honors of any sort unless literally commanded by the Pope.

If the Jesuit constitution has a military tone—and it has—that is quite natural. What other tradition did Ignatius know? Yet it is not altogether soldierly. From the start there was emphasis on scholarship, and that also was natural. The ten glittered with degrees. Some were even doctors of divinity. The founder might consider learning only a tool to be used for the love of God and mankind, but he could not and would not deny his followers the right to all available knowledge. As the years went on, the Jesuits were always to attract scholars, along with adventurers, explorers, missioners. Oddly enough, for all the fame of their intellectual achievements, they produced until recently few literary geniuses. Scientists, yes, biographers, historians, and writers on every subject under the sun, but no poets of stature except Southwell in the late sixteenth century, whose "The Burning Babe" even Dr. Johnson took the trouble to praise, and in the nineteenth, Gerard Manley Hopkins. In our own day we have a Teilhard de Chardin, whose mystical explanations of the unexplainable are poems in everything but form. It is possible that the activist tradition did triumph over the meditative and left no room for that intense self-preoccupation which poetry demands.

At the beginning of 1538, however, the ten were not even sure there was to *be* an order. They had won ordination and a grudging consent to get about their business with souls. But they lived in constant penury and with the incessant suspicion of authorities. One of the great Dominican preachers of the time, Fra Agostino (who was later to turn Lutheran) accused them of every sort of heresy, declared they were all fugitives from justice and ought to be burned at the stake. Had not a few powerful benefactors who admired the quiet holiness of the companions come to their defense with the governor, they might very well have been at least exiled.

Instead of that fate, they underwent one nearly as bad —a heartbreaking wait while Paul III mulled over whether or not he should let these ragged mendicants form a permanent society. After he saw their reputations as criminals and heretics cleared, he did finally appoint them instructors in Christian doctrine to the boys' schools of Rome. But the charter hung fire. Then in the winter of 1538, as

Brodrick says, "hunger and cold did even more than the Governor or Pope to win them what they wanted."

It was a terrible season, the worst in Roman memory. The storms, the killing cold, lasted from Christmas until the twenty-fifth of May, and famine and disease became endemic. Rodriguez, who, for all his oddities, was an admirable recorder of day-by-day events, writes that "everywhere in the streets and piazzas the poor lay huddled, frozen to the bone and dying abandoned in the night from hunger. There was no one to care for them, no one to shelter them, no one to take pity on their misery."

No one, that is, except the pilgrim fathers.

Those reliable heroes took on themselves the burden of the city's destitute. They put the sick into their own beds, begged straw pallets and food for the rest, and at times had as many as three or four hundred crowded into the ramshackle residence which was all they could afford. Any money bestowed on them they spent for the relief of tenement dwellers, "until not a farthing was left in the house." So spectacular were their efforts that even the Pope could no longer ignore them, and in 1540 he granted them the right to term themselves a genuine religious brotherhood.

"Jesuits" they never called themselves. They were the Company (later the Society) of Jesus. For a long while "Jesuit" was a nickname, a term of opprobrium applied to them by their enemies, of whom there were always sufficient. To this day we know that "jesuitical" is not a complimentary adjective. It smacks of all the things these first good men were not—of hypocrisy, dissembling, a belief that the end justifies the means. It is ironic that such a doctrine could have been attributed to any followers of Ignatius, a man who could not have lied to save his life or even, perhaps, his soul. His Spanish honor would not have permitted it any more than would his morals.

But then, I repeat, his life was all paradox. Spanish to the core, he spent his last fifteen years in Rome and always felt most at ease in Paris. He who had understood so little of the Reformation that he had to inquire about the identity of Luther, headed the forces which fought Catholic battles at the Council of Trent, where Protestantism was contained chiefly in northern Europe and where a compromise was hammered out for both combatants. The mystic who believed that to go unpersecuted, to become rich or influential was to deny the teachings of the Lord, lived to see his Society grow from ten to a thousand members, to become important and even fashionable. For in Italy, at least, it turned into rather a fad among the upper classes to attempt the Exercises.

What Ignatius would have thought of developments when, after Francis Borgia's great name had made the Society respectable, they began to own colleges and property and power, one cannot do anything except speculate. What he would have approved were the travels of his missionaries. Jesuit history is one of constant exploration and evangelism. Xavier, in Ignatius's lifetime, had got as far as Japan and died within sight of China, whose mysterious shores (having learned that the Japanese admired and copied everything important from that country) he yearned to visit. Other and later Jesuits roved the planet, usually as merciful camp followers of those European armies who were invading the New World. They went to all the Americas, to India, Africa, the Orient. No continent was too distant, no kingdom too dangerous, for them to reach.

The most celebrated of the explorers was Matteo Ricci, who as one of a group of three entered China in 1581 and almost turned that great country from Confucianism to Christianity. He had been especially trained for the undertaking, since the Jesuits saw what other Christians did not: that China was an enlightened culture superior in some ways to the European, and that only by meeting its officials on some elevated level would they be able to explain their message. Ricci and his two companions studied every modern device of science and entranced the governor of Kwangtung with the gift of a complicated and beautiful clock. Through this largesse Ricci became *persona grata* at court and was allowed to preach his doctrine, which he gracefully adapted to the Chinese tradition. He wore Mandarin robes and admitted that Confucius was a great teacher. After all, the Chinese have never insisted he was a god. Ricci made no attempt to swerve the people from their reverence for ancestry on which their religious life was, and still is, based. He simply argued to them that there was a nobler concept in Christian teaching which they could graft onto their own to everybody's benefit. He also brought with him maps and globes and astronomical instruments, which fascinated Chinese scholars and which they put to immediate use.

"Whatever is valuable in Chinese astronomical science," writes Charles Gutzlaff, a modern Protestant minister, "has been borrowed from the treatises of Roman Catholic missionaries."

Ricci was the first European to travel into the forbidden interior of China, and he made a Christian out of the most respected Mandarin at the Pekin court. Converts of every class followed him into the fold, and even after his departure their numbers kept swelling. In 1617 there were an estimated quarter of a million in one province alone.

The triumphs came to nothing. Priests of other establishments, coming now into China, denounced the Jesuits for what would presently be called their ecumenicism. It was charged that they taught that pagans were as good as anybody else (which charitable idea did not then inform Europe), and, since they had seen Ignatian priests joining in Confucian ceremonies, accused them of idolatry. When the tolerant Chinese found Christians squabbling among themselves, and ridiculing sacred ancestral beliefs, they repudiated the whole new religion and China was once more lost to the Western World.

It was such seed from which blossomed the suspicion among orthodox Catholics that perhaps the Jesuits were too lenient with Protestants and pagans. Any group ahead of its time runs into peril. And of course the Order's exploits in England, where they went so constantly but necessarily in disguise, and underground, also laid them open to the accusation of double-dealing.

No society is guiltless. By the time the company numbered thirty-six thousand members it was undeniably overpowerful. Nor were all its priests saints. They had intrigued at courts, they had fought Pascal in Port Royal, they had had their genuine scandals. They were human and learned and disciplined and vulnerable. And they were so influential that monarchs grew jealous of their power. In the eighteenth century this jealousy became paranoiac. Every king in Catholic Europe wished to dominate the Papacy rather than the other way around. The Jesuits, sworn to the Pope, opposed them. There is no space here to go into details about the struggle which resulted in the famous (or infamous as one sees it) Brief wrung from a timid Clement XIV in 1773, dissolving the Order entirely after seeing it suppressed earlier in Portugal, France, and Spain.

The Brief was supposed to have been read in every country in the world. But two important kingdoms, neither one Catholic, refused to publish it. They were Russia, under Catherine, and Prussia, ruled by Frederick the other Great. Those two powerful suzerains admired the Jesuits and their educational system and not only urged the ones already there to stay on but invited priests from other lands to join them. The paradox of Ignatius was still valid.

Many immigrated and kept the Society intact in exile. In such places as England and America the members did not disband but rather chartered themselves as organizations under another name. In America the twenty priests (who were then the only English-speaking Catholic clergy in the thirteen colonies) banded together as the Roman Catholic Priests of Maryland under the direction of Bishop John Carroll, brother of Daniel, the Signer. In England they called themselves the Gentleman of Stonyhurst.

Forty years later, at popular demand, the Pope issued a bull invalidating the suppression, and to Rome returned straggling elderly priests from all over the Continent. Many of the company had died in want. Some had taken

secular posts. But enough survived to pick up their work
where it had left off and to re-establish themselves as
an order.

I do not believe Ignatius would have been daunted by
the suppression. As I said, he welcomed persecution as a
sign of Christian grace. And he would have bowed to authority, like the Spanish soldier he was, but never deserted
his works of mercy and instruction.

It is a final paradox that he, the man of action, should
have been forced to spend the last fifteen years of his life
as an administrator rather than the foreign missioner which
was his heart's vocation. As we know, he sent others flying
about the earth. He remained a prisoner of duty in Rome.
He had not wished to be the first general of his Society.
Yet when the election was held for that office and when
he found that on both ballotings everyone's vote except
his own went to him, he accepted the burden with the
same cheerfulness and zeal he had brought to his wandering apostleship.

They were a worrisome fifteen years. Although he
watched the Order's membership almost miraculously expand, although talented novices flocked to him, he had
constantly to steer his company out of trouble. Other religious organizations continued to call them upstarts and
to charge them with heresy. In every country where he
set up foundations, political intrigue threatened their in-
dependence as an international and neutral society. Popes
remained suspicious of the Jesuit Rule, which departed so
abruptly from that of older orders. Even his own men had
to be kept in line, for in spite of their corporate brilliance
they were mortals with mortal faults and follies. Not all
were Xaviers, as full of obedience as affection.

Rodriguez, for instance, who had been made head of
the Portuguese province, proved so erratic in his activities
that Ignatius was forced to recall him to Rome. At the
Council of Trent, Bobadillo made his customary blunders
and had to be replaced, leaving Laynez and the young
Peter Canisius to do their remarkable work of conciliation

at that important conclave. But so strong was Ignatius's personality and so immense his industry and patience that he rescued his company from every storm that seemed about to shipwreck it.

And how much he got done! He founded and fostered schools and colleges, trained novices, watched over his students as he did the poor, preached, mediated, became a consummate diplomat, and wrote a stream of admonitory or comforting letters that would have done justice to Saint Paul.

In much of what he accomplished he was far ahead of his time. There is something exciting about watching the provincial Spanish captain turning into a man wide of outlook, fresh-visioned in every act. "Isn't it amazing," said Niebuhr in the same interview commenting on the Jesuits from which I have already quoted, "that this society, brought into being for the Counter-Reformation, should now become the organ for adapting the Church to all modern movements?"

To me it does not seem extraordinary. An Ignatius, alive today, and filled with the same large-heartedness and good sense that he exhibited after Manresa, would undoubtedly be leading the *aggiornamento* as he once inspired the forces of reasoned charity at Trent. Not only was he a genius; he also had a very modern mind. That it was a charitable mind goes without saying. Ignatius has been admired for centuries. He has not always been loved—he was too self-contained, too reticent to initiate the same wholesale affection that has been poured on Xavier and Peter Fabre—but there was enormous sweetness in him. One of his most endearing traits was to take on to his busy shoulders the penances he wished to spare his penitents.

He died in 1556, so suddenly that there was no time even for the last rites. Few men can have needed them less. And he must have died content to see most of his sons so obedient, his work so flourishing, yet still at hand always the hardships he welcomed. One cannot bring oneself to write after his name, "Rest in Peace." He who had loved struggle one can only hope is now being given in heaven the most difficult, the most demanding, the most Quixotic assignments that an obliging God can invent for His saints.

The Saints of Ireland

Behind every myth lies a truth; beyond every legend is reality, as radiant (sometimes as chilling) as the story itself.

I am reminded of this whenever I read a bit of Saint Patrick's Day oratory or hear an Irish-American chauvinist boast the ancient glories of Holy Ireland. "Land of Saints and Scholars" runs the famous brag, and one is inclined by bored habit to put it down as no more than defensive sloganeering.

Yet the truth and the fable go hand in hand. Little Eire was after Cromwell a "most distressful country" and is now merely a charming republic in the North Atlantic with a precarious balance of trade. Yet in her high day the glory was genuine. For several hundred years—from the fifth century until the tenth—in that green, garrulous, rain-washed, crotchety island the twin lights of learning and Christianity burned sweetly and steadily when they had gone out over Europe. Actual saints and real scholars preserved a persecuted faith, a classic but perishing literature, and by their immense efforts restored both to Western Europe when the era was ripe.

"While Pope Gregory the Great was reproving a Gallic Bishop for studying Latin grammar and poetry," writes the historian George Macaulay Trevelyan, "the Irish Christians were busy saving it for the world in their remote corner where Papal censure was unheard."

"Remote" is the key word. Ireland, having never been conquered (or civilized) by the Roman Legions, remained safely itself until the ravages of the Vikings in the ninth and tenth centuries and of the Englishman Strongbow (Richard Fitz-Gilbert de Clare, Earl of Pembroke) in 1170 reduced it to a vassalage. And by then her wandering missionaries had done their work in Scotland, in England, on the Continent. Europe was again Christian and knowledge had revived. The Dark Ages were over.

Oh, there were saints indeed in Ireland after her conversion in 432; saints numerous and as characteristically Celtic as shamrock. No other country ever owned more holy men per square mile, nor ones more native to the soil. Those good monks and nuns and acolytes who flocked like homing birds to monasteries and hermitages after Saint Patrick arrived were peculiarly products of their own eccentric shores.

Patrick is Ireland's patron. But, as nearly everyone knows, he was neither their first apostle (that honor belongs to Palladius) nor Irish by birth. He was a Romanized Christian probably from the lower Severn region in England, and proud of the Latin culture he had inherited. His father, Calpurnius, apparently owned his villa in the Roman style and was a government official. (It is interesting, in view of the current Catholic controversy over clerical celibacy, that not only was Calpurnius a deacon but *his* father was a priest. Evidently strict rules for an unmarried clergy had not yet taken root in the Western churches.) Irish raiders carried Patrick off in boyhood—about 403—to tend swine for a local chieftain. After his escape six years later he presumably studied for holy orders in either Tours or Auxerre, was made a bishop, and returned to preach the Gospel to the pagan people who had once enslaved him.

There would be nothing novel about his story (since, after all, a thousand saints have been missioners) except that he was so suddenly and so spectacularly successful. Never before or since in Christian annals has a country accepted the Word with such joyous alacrity. Ireland fell into Patrick's arms like a plum red for the harvest. There are, no doubt, logical reasons for his triumph besides personal zeal. We know there had been Palladius before him for a year or two. There may have been other preachers lost to historical sight who spoke of pious things to the unlettered tribes. And of course, although the cloudy land had gone unconquered, it was not entirely shut off from trade and rumor; so the Christian message may have come to a country not unprepared for it. Yet the actual conversion seems a sort of miracle.

He arrived in 432. By the time of his death in 461, the whole island had been altered from heathendom to an elated version of Christianity. Here and there an occasional tribal chief may have held out. We know the Druids grumbled before they vanished. But the mass of the people and leaders rushed into Patrick's fold like bridegrooms to the wedding feast. By 444 there was already a native clergy and an episcopal see in Armagh. There were churches, schools, the beginnings of a monastic life. And all this took place without so much as a single martyr, unless one excepts Patrick's charioteer, supposedly killed by an accident of archery during a journey.

I have mentioned that he brought with him the Word, and it seems to me that in the noun lies an explanation of his astounding victories. For it was the Word in both its figurative and literal sense. To tribes without a written tongue but for whom the bards had always been a principal caste, the gift of literature was as priceless as a hope of heaven. The genius of the Irish is that of language. Now they had offered to them not only salvation for the soul but sustenance for the mind in the shape of the classics and the Latin alphabet. We are not sure of Patrick's scholarship since we have from his pen only his *Confessions*, but like any self-respecting churchman of his day he must have traveled with books in his luggage—and those

books, both sacred and profane, became the treasures of
the island. It is as if the people had been starving for a
religion superior to their former belief in sea gods and
wood spirits, had been famished for reading. They could
not get enough of either. Books began to count as part of
the country's wealth like gold and cattle. Students spent
their lives copying them or writing others. For them kings
waged war and whole monasteries sprang up around a set
of volumes. I will describe later how possession of a book
was the axis upon which turned the career of Ireland's
most typical saint, gray-eyed Columba.

By the end of the fifth century the land pulsed like a
beehive with piety and learning. Tales say that there were
three hundred universities in the country. Even if we
discount Irish exaggeration and realize, also, that these
"universities" were probably nothing more than a group of
wattled huts built near a church, where the studious
prayed, chanted, illuminated manuscripts, and wrote out
their lessons, it does seem as if learning had become a
national obsession. Roaming scholars even began drifting
in from other countries to sit at the feet of Saint Finnian
or Saint Sechnall or Saint Ita—for women as well as men
took part in the educational blossoming. And all this went
on while Rome was disintegrating under the attacks of
Alaric, Gaiseric, and finally Attila. By 476, when Odoacer
deposed the last emperor, it was scarcely even a city and
Mediterranean culture lay dying. Only in tiny Ireland flourished the seeds of exuberance and hope.

There also flourished the saints. Their names are trum-
pet calls: Ciaran, Patrick's first disciple; Enda, Benen,
Brendan the mariner; Finnian the Educator; Adamnan the
biographer; delightful Bridget, whose hilarious charities
lost her a husband but gained her Paradise and who is
known still in Ireland by the exquisite title of "the Mary
of the Gael"; several Colmans; Kevin, Columbanus,
Ethne; Finbarr, the patron of Cork; a galaxy of others.
Most were monks and nuns. For like all young Christian

societies Ireland loved the monastic pattern, since in the monasteries resided the books.

It was a monasticism peculiarly native, one unlike either that of Egypt's desert or Benedict's strict Rule. Some things they had in common like simplicity, regard for the dignity of manual labor, and a naïve liaison with dumb beasts, which they sheltered and protected. (One need not believe literally that Colman of Galway kept for pets a cock, a fly, and a mouse, or that Kevin gave sanctuary to the wild boars when they were being pursued by hunters, to understand their reverence for all life; recluses everywhere have always made friends of small, frightened things.) But they differed in both their allegiance to the Latin Church and their asceticism. The latter was less rigorous than in other foundations.

It is said that on Iona, for instance, the monks were allowed straw pillows and mattresses; and meat and fish were abundant enough on the menu to keep the community strong for work in the fields. Beer also seems to have been a staple. "Public opinion," Father Ryan, the historian, comments wryly, "on the whole was against the teetotallers. The monk who drank nothing but water for thirty years was regarded as a great exception and his example was not followed with enthusiasm."

Along with their special version of fasting, they kept their Celtic adaptation of the liturgy, the Church Calendar, and the tonsure—shaving their heads across the pate from left to right instead of in the halo shape of European devotees. They celebrated Easter at a different time from Rome, and many a battle of words was waged over that date before the Synod of Whitby helped to bring them into line with Continental practices. Above everything else they retained their predilection for wandering. James Brodrick has called this urge "a divine restlessness of missionary zeal." And indeed without this restlessness there would have been no troop of voyagers to proselyte Europe, fanning out from Ireland to Iona, then to Lindisfarne,

Kent, Anglia, Cornwall, finally to Gaul and, some say, as far as Hungary and Denmark.

(Poor darlings, for all their persuasiveness and holiness, they had no talent for establishment. Their manner of evangelization was to preach, convert, and move on. Not until Augustine of Kent came from Rome to Canterbury with his Latin passion to organize did their churches become solidly a Church.)

Even the spirit of their monasteries was different from that of other countries. For Saint Patrick's disciples these good people may have been, but the religion they developed after him swerved in a direction he had not envisioned. Patrick was Rome's man; he was bred to orthodoxy, a strictly structured order. Those virtues did not suit the Irish temperament. They loved the Gospels. Monasticism they were eager to embrace, but their theology was as gentle as their behavior was sometimes impetuous. Pelagius is supposed to have been an Irishman. Whether he was or not, his heresy took deep root in Irish Christianity of the first centuries and lingered on there long after those fiery Church Doctors, Jerome and Augustine of Hippo, had won their war with his sweet, persuasive arguments. He taught that there was no such thing as Original Sin, that baptism was unnecessary for salvation, and that a virtuous pagan had as good a chance for heaven as a Catholic. (I wonder, in the light of today's ecumenism, if Pelagius will not some day be canonized.)

In any case, Patrick could no more make Romans out of his Gauls than the English were able later to transform them into tractable subjects of the British crown.

There must be something in that misty latitude which fosters at once fraction and puritanism. Those ancient saints demonstrate both characteristics. For example, Christian monastics have always sworn the three vows of poverty, chastity, and obedience. In sunnier climates, the first two have constituted the main stumbling blocks to holiness. In Ireland they seemed to give no trouble at all. Poverty was something to which they were accustomed.

Chastity they could accept without much struggle. We read of no Irish Augustine, praying "to be made chaste, but not yet," no devil-tempted Anthony wrestling with his animal nature. Only Columbanus comes to mind as one "afflicted by the flesh," and *he* spent most of his time out of Ireland. But what difficulty they had with obedience! So loosely organized were their communities that the inmates were continually hurrying off from their cells to rescue relatives from danger or stem a tribal riot. Or else, beset by too much companionship, they would remove themselves from the group and find seclusion like Ciaran, in a cave, or like Kevin, in a tree, to make their souls in peace. On behalf of the hermits, however, one must admit that the solitary life was proffered them (unlike the Desert Fathers) not as an apprenticeship but as a prize to be won by previous good works.

A host of them, such as Brendan, went traveling across strange oceans or, like Aiden, over nearby channels. And everywhere they went they brought the Good News. Trevelyan has painted an appealing picture of these rovers, calling them "the ardent, loveable, unworldly apostles of the moorland who tramped the heather all day to preach by the burnside at evening." And he adds, "Christianity has never, since its earliest years, appeared in a more attractive guise."

In one man among those heroes who thrived during the first ecstatic centuries is embodied all that is most characteristic of the Irish nature. I choose to tell his story rather than to list the accomplishments of the many. He was Columba, also called Columkill, "the Dove of the Church."

As usual with the early tales, his life is fossilized in legend. But enough of it remains to know its historical rudiments and I tell it as it has come down to us through Adamnan, who wrote his biography only thirty years after Columba's death, through Bede, and through tradition.

In person Columba was Irish as he was in spirit. "His eyes were the color of gray sea water"; he was tall, fair-skinned, dark-haired, with a voice—as one chronicler amusingly says—"so loud and melodious it could be heard a mile off." Supposedly he was a prince in his land, which ran rather to chieftains than sovereigns, for his father headed a branch of the Clan O'Neill, the island's most important family. Finnian the Educator was his first teacher. After Finnian had steeped him well in the classics, Columba was sent to study under "an aged bard" named Master Gemman. For, despite the fact that Ireland was by the sixth century both literate and Christian, tradition dies slowly, and the bards who had once been their country's sole historians, still possessed great power. They harped in the kings' halls and sat at the kings' tables. They presided over wars, weddings, funerals, celebrations; and at times they interpreted the laws. Columba was talented enough at verse-making to be admitted to the bardic order. But he opted in young manhood to become a priest and set about to establish his own churches and study centers.

However, he was yet no saint. In fact he was on his way to becoming a great sinner, and the cause of his sin was an overpowering lust for the written page. While paying a visit to his old tutor, Finnian the abbot, he was shown a magnificent manuscript chained to the stones of the library. It was one of the Gospels which Columba did not himself possess. "May I copy it?" he asked, and the request seems to us perfectly reasonable. Still, we cannot from our twentieth-century glut of books understand how tremendous a treasure that must have then appeared or how jealously it was guarded. At any rate, Finnian inhospitably refused. "You may read it a thousand times, but you may not copy it," he said. "It is unique."

Columba's hold on obedience was not very secure. To him Finnian must have seemed as ungracious and niggardly as he does to us. So, tempted by greed for the Word, our hero became a kind of thief. Night after night he crept illicitly downstairs to reproduce for himself the book which captured his imagination. When the "theft" was discovered, Finnian demanded back Columba's copy. He got nowhere, for when two obstinate Irishmen fall out there can be no meeting of minds. Finally the case was taken to Diarmuid, the High King, for his arbitration. Then came the famous decision which has for years so diverted historians.

"Both manuscripts belong to Finnian," said Diarmuid. "I follow the law. To every cow its calf and to every book its son book."

Wild with disappointment, Columba rushed back not to his monastery but to the headquarters of his clan. "Avenge me this injustice," he cried to the O'Neills.

Probably, since they were a lively lot, they enjoyed the excuse for a scrimmage. What followed, however, was not a local dustup but a genuine battle in which, says the tale, three thousand men were slain. The story goes on to describe Columba's belated horror when he saw the bodies of the fallen and realized he was responsible for their deaths.

It was then he swore his eternal vow. "I have committed a crime against God and Ireland. God I will pray to for the rest of my life. Also for the rest of my life I promise never again to look upon Irish shores."

So he embarked in his currach with twelve companions —all his relatives—and sailed across wild water until Ireland disappeared. When even on a clear day he could no longer make out its beloved shape, he stopped at an island and there began to build a chapel.

The island was Iona, in the Hebrides off the coast of Scotland. And the monastery he finally founded there was to be the longest-lasting and the most influential of all the Celtic abbeys. From that base he converted the pagan Scottish people of the mainland as well as the island. From it, too, the most successful of the pioneering monks went forth into Britain and the Continent. And also there Columba tamed his own defiant spirit into a gentleness still lauded by his countrymen. He taught scholars. He worked in the fields with his monks and protected the beasts and wild fowl, which, the legend tells, flocked about him.

He left Iona only once. His sole journey back to the Ireland he had forsworn was not a breaking of his vow. He made the trip by a ruse worthy of wily Odysseus—one typical, too, of the Irish who from earliest times had loved the uses of semantics.

In his absence the bards had become national nuisances. Overblown with pride of office, they had begun to drive hard bargains for their services. They meddled with politics, asked enormous prizes for presiding over a victory or a marriage, and in general paraded their power like officials—and poets—in every generation. The always prickly natives rose against them. At Tara they besought the King to put a stop to bardic misconduct.

The current occupant of the High Seat must have been a man as impulsive as the young Columba. Instead of merely reproving the bards he decided to exile them. "Off with you," he commanded. "We'll get along without you entirely."

Terrified by the sentence, the bards could think of nothing to do except enlist Columba on their side. "You are one of us," they told him by messenger. "Without you we perish."

Then came the problem. The saint in his tolerant solitude could realize better than the folk involved how Ireland would miss its praisers. Besides, he loved a well-turned verse. But how could he "look again on Ireland's shores" when he had made that solemn pledge?

Well, he could go without looking, could travel blindfolded to Tara. And that, of course, is what he did.

Once at court, he spoke with such eloquence to the gathering that they changed their stubborn minds.

"Meddlers and muddlers these bards may be," he reminded them. "But without their songs who will remember your glories? Who will harp the tales of your wars, the beauty of your women? You will lose your history."

So the poets were allowed to stay and Columba went back to Iona, blindfolded as he had left it, to live out his days in peaceful, God-fearing austerity.

Saints blossomed after Columba as they had burgeoned before him, some gentler, some even more boisterous than he, but all framed and formed by Ireland's climate. They were statesmen, poets, artists, almsgivers, artisans, explorers, evangelists. Unmolested by foreign influences, they fostered a delightful originality of conduct simply by grafting onto their native virtues of courage, hospitality, and a love of speech the Pauline graces of charity and respect for life.

The last recognized saint, Laurence O'Toole, died in 1180, just as Ireland's last High King, Rory O'Connor, was being routed by Strongbow. The "Irish problem" had begun. As the island's freedom waned, and no matter how holy her monks might have been, the country was too isolated from a revived Rome to let her good men be counted on the Calendar of a now Latinized church.

Iona's monastery, like those on the mainland, was destroyed by steel and flame. Of all that throbbing industry—the splendor of manuscripts lovingly illuminated, the artistry, the composing—only one relic of stature remains to raise our modern hearts. It sits now in the library of Dublin's Trinity College. There one can gape at it under its protective glass, stare at its pages that are turned one at a time and once a day. It is the superb Book of Kells and ranks among the most beautiful manuscripts in the world. It was discovered in County Meath amid the ruins of one of Columba's own early foundations.

Yet in spite of the destruction something more important than a single book has been salvaged from the rubble of a quirky civilization. We have the learning they preserved for us, the impact of their religious fervor. And we have the memory of their myth-encrusted lives. A thousand years of troubled darkness separates us from them. Yet now and then the night lifts and we see that they existed in the morning of the world. Forever about them glimmers (to quote a last time from Trevelyan) "the freshness and the light of dawn."

Heroes without Halos

One evening at the end of October, suburban America begins to twitter like an aviary. Underneath the fading maples, across leaf-strewn lawns, hordes of children flit giggling from house to house, masked, costumed, and in search of seasonal largess. Their voices enchant the night. And they too are enchanted by the one adventure of the year which is solely their own. It is Halloween. The trick-or-treaters roam on pilgrimage.

Few of them know the historical reason for the masquerade. Nor would many be interested in the background of this quaint holiday which in various fashions is observed throughout Christendom. Yet they are the preservers of a tradition. Their merry-making is a secularization of something once considered holy—a commemoration of the blessed dead. This is the eve of All Hallow's Day, which falls on November first and honors the memory of holy if anonymous souls.

The Roman Catholic Church, which initiated and still keeps the feast, is old and practical. It realizes that although there are thousands of saints entered in its Calendar, that list contains only a token number. Heroic virtue exists and has existed in the world far more luxuriously than the slate of the properly canonized would show. So long ago it set aside this anniversary in honor of those who served God and mankind without having achieved official sanctification.

An imaginative saint-watcher could keep the day all year around. Earth spawns virtue as often as it throws up evil; oftener, perhaps. No matter how cruel an era or bleak the times, true heroes arrive in it. They may or may not be religious believers but their existences follow the Gospel pattern. They comfort the afflicted, give to the poor, turn the other cheek, remain cheerful in adversity, lay down their lives for a friend. And the world loves to dwell on them. Humanity has an insatiable longing for good people to idolize. In them the ordinary man finds importance. His mortality is aggrandized and made honorable. The knowledge that great persons have done great deeds of kindness vanquishes his despair at the meanness of his own life, charges his daily atmosphere with vicarious glory.

All religious bodies honor in some way the souls who exemplify their moral teachings. There are Moslem saints, Hindu saints, saints among the followers of Confucius. After the Reformation in Europe many of the Protestant sects rejected as smacking of popery the old Christian Calendar with its thousands of ascetics and martyrs. Today they grow lenient and often pay homage to the truly universal among them. Indeed, the American Episcopal Church has recently published a list of saints in a small book with a long title—*The Calendar and Collects, Epistles, and Gospels for the Lesser Feasts and Fasts and for Special Occasions.* Printed there for use in the weekly liturgy are the names of many of the old familiar company who died and were enshrined before the Council of Trent. They range from Ambrose to the rather obscure Wulfstan, eleventh-century Bishop of Worcester, who, Butler tells us, "although not very learned, delivered the word of God so impressively and feelingly as to move his audience to tears." Francis of Assisi is there. So is Jerome. But included also, to my personal delight, are some brand-new members of the galaxy such as John Donne, George Herbert, William Wilberforce. Evidently the Anglican body is an accommodating group with literary and humanitarian leanings. Both Herbert with his mystical verse and Wilberforce, who spent a lifetime abolishing the slave trade in the British Empire, seem vigorous and less than whimsical choices—men who might be tapped by any devout committee. But that Donne, fashionable preacher at Saint Paul's who is so much better known to us for his erotic poetry than for his holiness should have his own Collect for March twenty-first gives me extreme pleasure, particularly since March twenty-first is my birthday. Thundering divine he may have been and, no doubt, in later years a serious penitent. Still, his election amuses me as much as if the Roman Curia had suddenly decided to canonize Bach.

Not that Rome would be so capricious. It, like other churches, alas, usually exalts its own. But it is tempting to speculate on which people of other communions, or of none at all, might now star in the Roman lists had they belonged to the Roman rite.

My speculation has nothing to do with denominational bias. It arises because the Catholic Church is the only great religious institution which rigidly and with legal ceremony examines those it would honor. (The orthodox churches have a canonization process but their operations are not very stringent.) It stands to reason that a religion so closely structured that it has categorized exactly seven deadly sins and seven capital virtues, and divided sins into those that are venial and those that are mortal, should also spend time and energy on defining canonization and working out its specifications so a watcher can recognize those who would qualify.

It was not always so. In the early days of Christianity the appellation "saint" meant something different from its current connotation. The word was applied by Paul and his successors to nearly all the Christian community and meant more or less "those who keep the faith." The title was granted automatically to martyrs, of whom there were a host in the first few centuries. Later sainthood took on overtones of local worship and became a matter of popular and civic acclaim. Any outstanding personality who was pious enough to gain attention from the population or who had perhaps guarded their military interests was apt to get into the liturgy, as Charlemagne and Olaf did.

Then as the Latinization of the Church proceeded to take command in Europe the proliferation of local cults began to worry the hierarchy. Too much became legend, too many "saints" confused the Calendar. By the tenth century the pope had established some sort of central control over canonizations and by 1181 Innocent III had reserved all future rites for the Holy See. But it was not until 1634 that the full process emerged formally with its intricate detail, its scrupulous inquiries into the life of the nominee, its judges, advocates, trials, verdict, and final triumphant proclamation. Since then it has been nearly as hard to boost a candidate up the beatific stairway as for the rich man to make his way to heaven. It requires public pressure, adequate funds (for amassing testimony), and sustained patience. The wheels of the Vatican grind slowly. But influential voices in the Church are being raised in favor of returning to the old ways of local acclaim, and such non-Catholic candidates as King and Schweitzer are already in nomination.

It is also necessary that the person under consideration have been widely recognized in his or her lifetime as a virtuous being. For one is reminded by Donald Attwater, who has written a brief dictionary of holy people, that "a man or woman is not made a saint by canonization. Canonization in which the voice of the people at large is often still a very powerful factor . . . is an authoritative declaration that such and such a person was a saint in his lifetime."

Which implies that the candidate has to have been *successful.* He has to have been heard of as far as Rome, preferably the world over. And his cause must have conformed to orthodox ideals. Blaise Pascal was a celebrity and one of the most devout Catholics of his era, a universal genius, a man who in his middle years turned as mystical as Teresa and mourned the time he had wasted on inventions instead of prayer. But he had the misfortune to espouse a hopeless cause, that of the Port Royal rebels. So for all his passion, all his enormous literary gifts, all his service to Christianity and the poor, he remains outside the Calendar and half a heretic. Heresy is like treason. If it triumphs none dare call it heresy; if it fails it brings down all its advocates.

On the other hand, it ought to be easy to halo John the XXIII. So long as the *aggiornamento* maintains its hold on the mind of the Church, he will be a certified hero, looming so large in men's hearts that the most reactionary of councils can scarcely deny him his virtuous accolade.

Eminence, success, financial backing for a long siege of the authorities—those are the secular requisites. No wonder so few saints are canonized in modern times unless they happen to have been spectacular martyrs. Since the seventeenth century the candidates most frequently honored have been either heads or revered members of religious orders. An order has a long memory. It has the continuity, the organization, and usually the funds to keep its case before the proper committees.

Because I realize the factors that enter into the canonization procedures, I do not waste my imagination on those whom I consider saints by definition but whom perhaps only I have watched at work. I like to count through the famous people who, as I said, might well have been elevated by Rome had they belonged to the Roman communion. And the first name that occurs to me is that of Florence Nightingale. She was wildly successful, world-esteemed, and she owned the kind of nature that, had she been a believing Catholic, would almost certainly have led her into founding a nursing order. A more typical lady abbess never lived. She had inborn authority. Her personal charm was enough to draw disciples about her and convert them into a disciplined band. And she had the steely will, the singlemindedness, of all great reformers.

"It was not by gentle sweetness and womanly self-abnegation," writes Lytton Strachey, one biographer who did not adore her, "that she brought order out of chaos in the Scutari Hospitals; that from her own resources she had clothed the British Army, that she had spread her dominion over the serried and reluctant powers of the official world; it was by strict method . . . by rigid attention to detail, by ceaseless labour, by the fixed determination of an indomitable will."

Of course. Mr. Strachey was attempting to tarnish the image of the Lady with the Lamp; he succeeded in merely characterizing genius. Some saints are completely lovable; others intimidate by their very force, and probably none, as I have said, has been altogether cozy. Who can feel wholly comfortable in the presence of capabilities larger than life size?

Florence Nightingale was one of the most remarkable women who ever lived. In her long lifetime, twenty years of it spent in bed, she worked for humanity with something near ferocity. Nothing—not a difficult family, entrenched bureaucracy, stupid generals, or stubborn cabinet ministers —was sufficient to stand in her whirlwind path. Although in girlhood she was devout and conscience-questioning, she never became a religious searcher in a real sense. At one time she thought of turning to Rome but was discouraged first by her friend Cardinal Manning, then by her obsession with remaking English hospitals. Yet I see her in a different era and climate as another but greater Mother Jahouvey, a mother superior with bishops instead of poor overworked Sidney Herbert taking her commands and viceroys rather than Queen Victoria applauding her progress. She had a vocation as genuine as Catherine's or Rose's. It simply, in an Anglo-Saxon country, expressed itself in a different fashion.

Her story, familiar though it is, never ceases to astonish. We see her first as the pretty "Flo," rich and well-born, confiding to God in her early diaries that she felt He had called her to something more important than doing the flowers for the drawing room and catering to Mama, Papa, and her hysterical sister, Parthe. Then came the debutante, "adoring" balls and knowingly turning the heads of young men, none of whom she could ever bring herself to marry. And there is the agonized woman, getting on toward thirty, stifling in her idle, upper-class nineteenth-century atmosphere. There was never perhaps another period in which women were so compassed about by the rules of good breeding, by what was or was not permitted them. She struggled. She floundered. And she suffered agonies of depression when she realized that although, as she wrote, "the first thought I can remember, and the last, was nursing work," she was being deprived of the profession she longed for.

Her family insisted that her duty was at home. Her intellect, her magnificent talents, told her otherwise.

"My God! What is to become of me?" she wrote in despair after the last of a series of foreign travels (the Victorian's remedy for everything from neuroses to tuberculosis) had reduced her to nothing but misery.

In a Catholic country she could have fled to a convent. A Miss Florence Nightingale had no such sanctuary. All she understood was that her place was in a hospital, that she was happy only when she was nursing invalids, the more indigent the better.

But one has to recall what public nursing meant at that time. Hospitals were not only primitive and unsanitary; they were squalid beyond belief. The poor went there not to recover but to die under a roof. Nurses were usually prostitutes or drunkards, often both. Yet the yearning to run such an institution and to make it over according to her own acquired ideas of medicine and hygiene began to haunt her more and more.

She won through at last, but not until she was nearly thirty-four. And her victory entailed as much melodrama as a mystery novel. She intrigued with powerfully placed friends, like Sidney Herbert and his sympathetic wife. She hid her purposes from her parents. By stealth she studied everything to do with nursing practice and by subterfuge managed to spend a few months in Germany at a model hospital run by a Pastor Flieder. She braved her sister's storms, her mother's resentment, even the disapproval of society for this rebel daughter whose outrageous ambition it was to mingle with the wretched of London in unsuitable surroundings. In Lima or Siena her behavior would not have sounded odd; only in England and in her own century did Miss Nightingale appear a mad adventuress.

Her first triumph was a compromise. She took charge of a charitable hospital for indigent gentlewomen in Harley Street run by a committee of society women—or rather, misrun. All sorts of restrictions hedged her about, but problems only whetted her appetite for administration. In a brief time she had reorganized the nursing care, trained a corps of women helpers, arranged all on a sensible and efficient basis. She then might have gone on only to re-form such decorous projects—now becoming stylish as good works for the idle—had not disaster struck Britain. (Disaster has often been the opportunity of saints.)

England entangled herself in the Crimean War. Of all her wars this was the most mismanaged. Not only were the generals less than brilliant; the whole effort was hamstrung by red tape and out-of-date orders. Generals lost battles and bureaucracy lost its head. What was worse was that no provision had been made for the care of the wounded who began streaming in from the field. Fortunately the country then had a telegraph system, and by that means stay-at-home Englishmen began to hear what was happening to its defeated forces. Up went a spontaneous and public cry for civilian help, and Miss Nightingale was quick to answer it. Here was work on a scale to match her genius.

Again against opposition but supported by the Herberts and their circle, she got her by now imperious way, and with a small band of trained women embarked for what was to be her most famous achievement. Unlike many of the volunteers who traveled East—often as mere sightseers

—she went prepared. Funds both public and private had been put at her command, and she used them to buy stores of medicines and bandages which, although the government had promised they would be available, intuition told her she would have need of. But nothing had prepared her for the absolute destitution she found in her first hospital at Scutari. There had been complete breakdown in official competence. The hospital was a cold and filthy barracks. The only nurses were a few convalescent soldiers able to keep on their feet, the doctors so scarce and so bound by red tape that they scarcely dared prescribe for a patient. There were almost no beds, blankets, shirts, medicines. Even the food was in short supply and close to inedible.

The world knows and has always rejoiced in the deeds of valor that Miss Nightingale performed in the Crimea, but sentimentality has made the Lady with the Lamp her chief role; she is thought of as moving through the aisles among the ill, plucking up their courage. And when she had a little time, she did encourage the wounded and the dying. But that gesture as ministering angel is the smallest part of her role. She who had to work with generals became herself a general, in tight command of her forces. Working with doctors, and being scrupulous to follow their orders, she became as good a physician as any of them. She was quartermaster, provisioner, dietitian, architect of physical changes in the wards, housekeeper, ruler and arbiter not only of her temperamental band of lady helpers but of artisans and carpenters and orderlies. She turned diplomat. And incessantly she wrote letters, setting forth the state of affairs at the hospitals and begging for more and more financial aid. What she accomplished was a miracle—the kind of miracle saints demonstrate oftener than levitation or the stigmata.

The war and her triumphant part in it were, as I said, what made her world-famous. But it was the beginning, not the end, of her achievements. She returned to England an invalid, but nothing could persuade her to rest. She was haunted by the ghosts of Scutari, and what she had determined on was nothing less than the reform of the entire Army medical system, even of the War Office itself. And in the course of her amazing ninety years that is what she did. She reformed all hospitals, military and civil. She made nursing as a career not only respectable but inviting. She was an inspired revolutionary whose influence outlasted her century and whose rules for nursing standards and dietary norms are pretty much in force still. Before her image changed from that of national heroine to superannuated legend, she effected alterations in the concept of the British army. The Whig idea of an enlisted man as someone subhuman who would not appreciate care if he received it was succeeded by the Kiplingesque ideal of the undereducated but authentic hero. By her counsel cabinet ministers changed their plans, and when military barracks were built in India they embodied her notion of architecture, which took the climate into account. She was a power everywhere in the world. The Queen doted on her, the Prime Minister consulted her, and foreign emissaries would not leave England without an audience.

That in pursuit of her goals she cast aside the attachments of family life, friendships which could not advance her projects, and her own health, meant no more to her than they have meant to many of the sanctified. And I am convinced that, whether she worked for her somewhat amorphous God or only for humanity, she deserves her aureole. I cannot believe that a church of which she might have been a devotee would have done anything except reward her efforts.

To an older and simpler design of blessedness belongs another of my candidates. He is in many ways the most beloved figure of this era, the Mahatma Gandhi. Mahatma means "great-souled," and even his enemies could scarcely deny him the appellation. He was a reformer who influenced the world and still influences it, since he united the twin movements of revolution by nonviolence and "civil disobedience." But for all that he shook the planet, and did it in a modern age, his spiritual aspirations fit naturally into the antique pattern of ascetics and solitaries. The Desert Fathers would have understood him, and the Celtic saints would have called him one of theirs. Even the fiery Augustine might have found him compatible, different in temper though they were. For we reach the soul of Gandhi not only through his work but in his autobiography, which might well be called, like older books of this sort, his Confessions.

It is a fascinating document, recording as it does not only the acts of his life and the reasons for those acts, but contemplation, reflection, and some self-berating. Again, as in the case of Augustine, his sins do not seem very wicked to us, but he regrets them, regrets all that bound him to worldly passions. And like others who demand virtue in their lives he was never satisfied with his accomplishment. "There can be no room for self-praise" he writes. "The more I reflect and look back on the past, the more vividly do I feel my limitations."

He was born in Porbandar, India, into a caste of businessmen who had come up in the world to the estate of government office. Once more Augustine-like, he gives credit to his mother for having early implanted in him ethical and moral yearnings. His was the usual schoolboy saga of shirked lessons and vague rebellions against authority, and he accuses himself of being both an idler and a coward. At thirteen he was married. Although the match lasted for more than sixty years, he never reconciled himself to such a "preposterous" custom as child marriage and later fought to end it. He says that it waked his "carnal appetites" too soon, and to the finish of his days he blamed himself for being so physically in love with his child bride that he neglected his obligation to "educate her mind." And he notes quaintly that being sent to study in England at nineteen gave him "a long and healthy separation" from her. What she felt about being deprived of a husband is not recorded.

In London he studied law at the Inns of Court, worked

to overcome his congenital shyness, learned to dance, and became a dandy. A friend described him there as being most fashionably dressed in morning coat and ascot, patent-leather shoes with spats, carrying gloves and a silver-mounted cane. He was not very happy in England in spite of his dressiness, but he credits the experience with giving him the background for his later campaigns and reforms.

After graduation he returned to India, failed to make a prosperous living, and went to South Africa, where prospects among the Indian colony there were reported promising. And it was in South Africa that the incident occurred which turned his mind toward liberating his people from British rule.

He boarded a train from Durban to Pretoria with a first-class ticket. On the way, an officious South African came into the compartment. It seems nearly unbelievable to us now (and must then have seemed so to Gandhi) that there could be extremists so ignorant that they should take offense at having to travel with a "colored man" who was not only a gentleman and scholar but descendant of a race whose civilization antedated theirs by thousands of years. Yet we know such things continue to happen.

Gandhi was bewildered. "But I have a first-class ticket," he protested.

"Then you've wasted your money," said the conductor when he was summoned. "Coloreds ride in the van."

The proud little Hindu was forced into a third-class section of the train without daring even to open his luggage for an overcoat to warm him in those high altitudes. Throughout that shivering night he pondered the inequalities of a political system which could reduce him and his fellows to such mental and physical misery. He wondered where his duty lay. Should he return to India or stay on in Africa? Heroically he decided to stay, and not only to stay but to organize an Indian party there to fight discrimination. The decision would not seem so valorous had he not been shy, introverted, and uneasy with public affairs.

It was the beginning of his campaign for Indian rights which embraced eventually human rights everywhere, including the untouchables of his own religion. His success was great. Yet it is not success that gives him saintliness, although that permits us to see him clear. It is his method of arriving at it. His adventures seem outward ones, but the struggle was interior. In order to remake his world he must remake himself. Only justice could right injustice.

"To see the universal and all-pervading Spirit of Truth face to face," he was to write, "one must be able to love the meanest of creatures as oneself. And a man who aspires after that cannot afford to keep out of any field of life. That is why my devotion to Truth has drawn me into the field of politics, and I can say without the slightest hesitation and yet in all humility that those who say religion has nothing to do with politics do not know what religion means."

As a practicing Hindu he would, in any case, have rejected violence. But more than that, violence outraged his principles. Authority must rise from spiritual ascendancy. It sounds rash—a young, inexperienced man whose career had so far been mediocre to set his ambitions so high as to try converting a nation. But saints have always had a sort of holy effrontery which comes, no doubt, from lack of personal vanity. They do not say to themselves, "This or that is impossible and will make me appear ridiculous." They say, "I will do the work of God." In that way Gandhi resembles Ignatius. Both perfectly humbled themselves, they had goals that were very wide. And they both shook their worlds more mightily than had they been warriors.

Prayers, fasts, exhortations, and what turned out to be a genius for organization—those were Gandhi's weapons. With his loincloth and his spinning wheel (symbol of India's rural power) he became an international figure whom governments feared even while they imprisoned him. Put him in jail and he emerged more dominant than

ever. Silence him and everyone heard him more clearly.
His life became a series of happy martyrdoms and ended
at last in a genuine one at the hands of an assassin who
slew him out of the belief that the Mahatma had connived
with the British at partitioning India and Pakistan. Earth
mourned.

He does not need a nimbus to make him a saint. The
world has already awarded it to him. But I like to think of
him now in Paradise ecumenically rubbing elbows with
the blessed of all faiths. There cannot be one of the list
who does not recognize him as a dear companion.

To that same company belongs John Wesley, one of the
most interesting of historical figures. He is more enigmatic
than either Gandhi or Florence Nightingale, more complicated as man and reformer, his aims less clear at first
to both himself and his followers. But he, too, in his time
changed, if not the world, at least England.

Historians insist that had it not been for his evangelization of the English lower classes the contagion spread by
the French Revolution might have crossed the Channel.
Riots and abortive rebellions were not unknown in that
century of Hanoverian rule. And God knows the poor of
England had enough to rebel against—meager wages, an
entrenched aristocracy which ignored their plight, ignorance, and a penal system which punished the debtor in
the same fashion as the criminal. Nor did the established
Church give them either help or hope. It was the era of
the huntin', shootin', bottle-a-day parson who had entered
the ministry not on account of a vocation but because it
offered a gentlemanly way of making a living. Often it
was the only profession open to a younger son, and he got
his post through family influence, embracing "religion" as
casually as he might have bought a commission in a regiment. Even when the rector was a good man he was alien-
ated from the mass of the people, and the churches often
stood empty except in such villages as those where the
squire set an example to his tenantry by sitting in his pew
of a Sunday and reading the Lesson. There were multi-

tudes in the cities and the countryside who knew no more of the Christian message than did an inhabitant of Timbuctoo.

That church and people finally came to terms with one another was due almost entirely to the impact upon both of Wesley's Methodism.

The same historians who credit Wesley with warding off bloody revolt are apt now to blame him for letting the System continue as he found it, for reconciling the indigent to their lot rather than inciting them to alter it. Patience and obedience as virtues have gone out of style in this day.

But hindsight is often blind. Nobody wins a civil war, and it was well that England had none. What John, and his brother, the tuneful Charles, managed to do was to change the attitude of the upper classes toward those less fortunate—to show that hordes need not be unruly nor ordinary working men stupid and drunken once someone dangled the hope of heaven before them. It is true that the brothers comforted wretches in prison without condemning the laws that put them there; that task was left to Oglethorpe, and even he merely offered them transportation to Georgia. It is also true that while writing and preaching against the slave trade they left to Wilberforce the glorious duty of abolishing it altogether. But biographers forget that in the middle of the eighteenth century there were enough evils to combat without taking on an economic battle which, in any case, would have yielded to no single person's effort.

I admit I am prejudiced. I love John Wesley as I love Augustine and Ignatius and Thomas Aquinas and Teresa. I love him for his cheerfulness and wit, for the justness of his nature, for the manner in which his sympathies enlarged through the years until he who had been in his youth in danger of being a prig became the most ecumenical and Pauline of apostles. I love him for his congenital charity, which could believe wickedness in no one. And I love and pity him for his lifelong struggle against his real vocation for celibacy. If ever a saint was destined for the single life it was John. But as a good Protestant he fancied that celibacy bore a popish taint. Also his charm as well as his chosen mission to bring the Method into every life drew to him young and beautiful women from whom he kept retreating in a one-step-forward, two-steps-backward kind of waltz, protesting that they had his complete affection but never bringing the matter to the sticking point. After he had turned well past forty and after Charles' marriage, he out of duty made an arranged match with a termagant. The union, if one can call it that, was unhappy in the extreme. The pair lived together for two or three years, all of them miserable, and lived apart for more than a score. It is pleasant to read that after he had shed his difficult spouse he set up house with his sister Patty and that in old age he knew domestic coziness.

But that coziness came about after years of contention and misadventure. All saints are converted from something, usually a carnal life. Neither John nor Charles (who was so much his alter ego for twenty years that one cannot write about one without mentioning the other) needed to repent of "chambering and wantonness." They grew up in piety and came of a devout family. Their father, Samuel, was Rector of Epworth and was more worthy than most, although he followed custom sufficiently to be often an absentee pastor more interested in getting his poetry published than in filling his pulpit. But the mother, Susanna, in spite of the burden of bearing eighteen children in nineteen years, brought up those that survived in strictly religious ways. Most of England might be peopled by an indolent and less than dedicated clergy, but at Epworth Parsonage all was decorous and prayerful.

So when John Wesley went to Oxford he had no need to feel remorse for a debased youth. What he had to recover from—and it took him a long time—was an excess of prudery, a too scrupulous habit of examining his own soul. And he was abetted in this by the influence of William Law, whose famous tract *A Serious Call to a Holy and Devout Life* fell into John's hands shortly after he came to the university. Law was one of the kindest of men, but his book the young student took without a grain of Attic salt. He determined to form his life upon Law's precepts, his Method for attaining a state of Christian devotion. Charles followed where his stronger brother led, and presently the two were joined by a few others who called themselves Methodists and practiced the most ascetic of daily routines —rising at four, praying, fasting, attending to good works such as prison-visiting, and proselytizing in their scant spare time.

The brothers and their group might have gone on quietly with such simple acts had not a new sort of adventure suddenly called them. They were suggested to Oglethorpe as ministers and secretaries to accompany him and his shipload of debtors newly released from jail on their way to the Colony of Georgia. For everyone concerned—Oglethorpe and the brothers, that is—there could not have been an unhappier choice. John was too severely Anglican to suit the brawling colonists; Charles made an inept secretary. A Wesleyan rigidity was to reside always in Charles. In John it gave way, late but fully, when he discovered at last, after returning defeated to England, what was to be his real mission. It was to carry the Word of God to ordinary people, to the abandoned, those whom the Church as such neglected. Again enlisting Charles on his side, he set about his journeyings as an itinerant preacher, which he was to continue for a very long lifetime.

At first all they found was difficulty. The local clergy resented their efforts; the magistrates called down the law upon their heads although they were breaking none. An easily aroused citizenry pelted them with eggs and rocks. They were accused of being heretics, traitors.

England was a restless country in the mid-eighteenth century. Abortive rebellions made the land fearful—fearful of any new religious movement or of any return to the ancient monarchy which the Georges had supplanted but not completely uprooted. In the Forty-Five Rebellion the little Methodist gatherings were accused of plotting the return of the Stuarts. During the later Gordon Riots mobs turned on them as savagely as they did on the poor, cowering Catholic minority. It is to John's eternal credit that in spite of personal danger he wrote a tract against papist-baiting even while stoutly asserting his own strong Protestantism.

But little by little, and in spite of all opposition, the movement began to succeed. The excitement and fervor of John's sermons, the sonorous music of Charles' hymns, worked a kind of miracle on those who came to listen. And they came from everywhere and went anywhere the brothers led them. Denied a church in London, the missionaries preached in a foundry which later became famous as a Methodist landmark. Driven from pulpits in the country, they spoke in the open air—in lanes, woods, fields. Gradually they influenced people of means who could help them in their apostleship. Little by little they became respectable. But they never wavered a hair's breadth—at least John did not—from their goal, which was to convert and educate the poor. That small saint, so cheerful that he was daunted by no hardship, so affectionate that he could hardly find fault even with his enemies, did in the end make converts by hundreds of thousands on both sides of the Atlantic. And in making converts he also gave many a better and more comfortable life than they had had before. For along with the Gospel he preached such fundamental virtues as sobriety and thrift. And even in those times a working man who earned his weekly wages and spent nothing in public houses was able, generally, to provide for his family. Material excellence often has its material reward.

It is ironic that neither John nor Charles ever intended to set up a schismatic religion. Each considered himself always a loyal priest of the Church of England. Charles was almost fanatical on the subject, and the rift between the two which lasted for some years came about not only over John's marriage (of which Charles hysterically dis-

approved) but because of John's casual way with established doctrine. For the older that extraordinary man grew,
the larger and larger became his tolerance and the more
ecumenical his spirit. Most of us narrow after middle age.
John Wesley at eighty-four held the human race in higher
regard than he had at twenty-four, and forgave it more
abundantly for its transgressions. As for Church regula-
tions, he kept them on a loose rein.

Were there no ratified ministers to speak God's message,
to spread the Method? Then he would use honest trades-
men, carpenters, artisans to convey the Word. Did the
congregations grow restive at service where the long sermon was enlivened only by an intoning choir? He would
urge the audience to join in to make a joyous noise unto
the Lord. So all of Charles' hymns, many of which he
composed on horseback, singing like a bird from the sad-
dle, were incorporated into Sabbath doings. Perhaps
communal singing, an innovation in that day, was one
reason for Methodist success in Wales, most musical of
northern countries. In the end he went so far as to do
away with Episcopal ordination—although only out of necessity. Hearing that the American Colonial ministers had in
large part fled the Revolution, that flocks were left without
shepherds, he took on the highly unorthodox business of
ordaining priests himself to send abroad. He had for many
years been using laymen in England to carry on pastoral
duties; now he let them head parishes. Finding them won-
derfully useful in all ways, he established a Committee of
a Hundred of the most faithful to oversee his churches'
work, and to this day the Hundred administer Methodist
affairs.

Dear man, he had little to repent in old age, since, as I
said before, his had never been a dissipated life. But he
repented just the same, admitting to an earlier straitness
of viewpoint, which he perpetually regretted. And he
repented so wholesomely that although he had always
stood stoutly against Rome, when Charles' youngest son
became a Roman Catholic against his father's bitter op-

position it was John who wrote to the young convert, "I care not who is Head of the Church, provided you be a good Christian. . . . What is spoken in love will be taken in love."

He even went so far in changing his puritan attitude that, although he had once preached fiercely against the theater as a frivolous diversion, he made sure to attend the musicales given by Charles' two talented sons—even staying up for the occasions far past his usual bedtime.

He was a reformer as genuine as Luther, if less belligerent. Unlike Master Martin, he did not set out at first to challenge authority, but in the course of his teachings he *did* challenge it shakingly and reformed the Establishment. The Church of England was forced to put off its lethargic and ingrown habits and open its doors to those with whom it had lost touch; was made to examine its conscience, to make sure its clergy were as nearly as possible men of God. He even forced the state to institute reforms in its treatment of the grossly underprivileged, of the wrongly imprisoned, of the sick and the orphaned. And he taught his enemies to admire him, if for the wrong reasons. After all, both landlords and lords of the realm had to admit that out of injustice grew riots and disorder, that some attention to the poor made for a more peaceable country.

It was John Wesley's good fortune to live long enough to find himself—as Mabel Brailsford, his not uncritical biographer, writes—"the best loved and most respected figure in the kingdom. Wherever he went, crowds of disciples and admirers, with troops of children, would meet him as he drove through the entrance of town or village."

And it touches me that old Lord Oglethorpe, who had thought in Georgia that the young stick, Wesley, would never make much stir in the world, at a chance meeting impulsively bent down to kiss his hand.

Gandhi, Wesley, Florence Nightingale—surely hearts beat more quickly when we contemplate them and their greatness. They happen to fill the technical requirements for canonization; but I could name a dozen others who equally deserve enshrinement, who also help the race feel honor in the fact of being human.

For mankind needs the brave and just. All heroes appeal to us, but those who add nobility of mind to valor force us to venerate them. Without saintly example to feed the imagination, we starve. In an increasingly irreligious age we begin to adopt secular saints, people who have served as catalysts for some public cause. Those thousands who every day stand silent in the portico of the Lincoln Memorial, stirred and humbled by that brooding stone figure, the multitudes who trudge up the slope of Arlington Cemetery to bow their heads at the Kennedy grave—they are as true adorers as the crowds who in Italy or Spain throng to kiss the relic of some ancient blessed. We mourn the memory of Martin Luther King and invoke him constantly. The New Left turns to Che Guevara for its odd idea of sanctity. And we all do exactly what a medieval citizenry once did, especially to its martyrs—we try to adorn them with legend true to the spirit if not always the letter of their accomplishments. I, for one, have no objection to a touch of myth. Greatness is not really harmed by embroidery but made significant.

So let us, by all means, tell over the names of our favorites among the heroes of earth and heaven, keeping a kind of All Hallows continual memorial for the best and bravest among us. These people give us hope, and may, as I said at the beginning, at length give us a little grace.

Afterword

It would be pretentious of me to compose a formal bibliography of source materials for this book, which is not and never was designed as a work of scholarship. Moreover, my references came to me from so many places, from such diverse reading, that a list would weary the mind. For, in addition to utilizing certain favorite histories of my own and those I could obtain through the good offices of libraries, I have, over the years spent producing this piece of writing, seized on every mention of saints that I found in magazines, newspapers, parish bulletins, editorials, essays, tracts, and anthologies.

But readers might like to know where I drew my basic information, and I confess a large part of it came from that famous, learned, and hortatory set of volumes, Alban Butler's *Lives of the Saints*. Indeed, I may well be the only nonreligious in America to have read through the four heavy tomes (and I mean the adjective in both its literal and figurative senses) from beginning to end. Those who have never consulted Butler ought to learn a little about the man who for over two centuries has edified the pious and tired the ears of girls in convent schools.

Butler was an eighteenth-century English cleric educated in France and in residence there most of his life. The reason for his exile is a historic one. He was born in North-

amptonshire in 1710, and during the span of his existence,
which ended in 1773, the Penal Laws were much in force
in England. Not only were English Catholic gentlemen
barred from educating their sons at home, but any priest
found saying mass in the kingdom was liable to life im-
prisonment. I must add that liberal-minded English juries
were slow to convict such culprits, but it *was* nearly impossible to remain Roman Catholic in those days without harsh
penalties. Only a few powerful nobles were able to flout
the laws and retain the old faith. The one interlude during
which Butler spent any amount of time in his homeland
was when he was household chaplain to the Duke of Nor-
folk, whose estates formed a little Catholic island, insolently
maintaining itself in the midst of a sea of Protestantism.
Of course, prejudice can work both ways. The Norfolks
remained so unmovedly Catholic throughout the Reformation and afterward that even today, I am told, it is difficult
for a non-Roman to acquire property in the borough of
Arundel, the present Duke's domain.

So young Alban went to Douay to school, stayed on in
France as a secular priest, and ended his days as president
of the College of Saint Omer. But he never thought of himself as anything but steadfastly English. So when he discovered early in his career that there existed in the English tongue no definitive reference work on the officially
canonized—in fact, that the last important book on the
subject of saints in that language was a translation of
The Golden Legend put into print by Caxton himself—the
young man set out to repair the gap. *The Lives of the
Saints* took most of his adult life and was published first
in London sometime between 1756 and 1759.

It is ponderous writing. Not only is its prose that of the
stately mid-eighteenth century; it also has a floridity of its
own drawn from the Latin that Butler studied and the
French that he spoke. Moreover, he thought of his books
as being primarily used to assist religious devotions. Each
Life is followed by a moral or a homily. And although he

did do an enormous amount of research, he is not without credulity; legends and miracles abound in his pages.

Fortunately in this decade two men more up-to-date and more scholarly than the Reverend Butler, Donald Attwater and the Jesuit Herbert Thurston, "edited, revised and supplemented" Alban's majestic labor, pruning it of verbiage, hearsay, and mythology. Even their version does not make light reading, but it is as authoritative as any book about saints which includes those exalted in the earlier days of Christianity can be.

That, then, was my general reference book. But I fear I used it in a manner of which none of the three gentlemen concerned with its composition would approve. For I read it all, but the notes I took concentrated on what was either picturesque or amusing about my subjects. I can only hope that dear studious Alban, who used to be seen walking down the street "with a book in either hand" and who was as devout as he was industrious, is not too horrified at the frivolous uses to which his pious labors have been put.

Many other books that I found valuable made far less onerous reading. G. M. Trevelyan's *History of England* is delightful both as history and as narration. Helen Waddell's *Beasts and Saints* and *The Desert Fathers* should enchant the casual reader and were of immense help to me. So were the writings of James Brodrick, S. J., particularly *The Origin of the Jesuits,* in which even the footnotes are witty. That book was my principal source for the chapters on Ignatius and Francis Borgia, although for the former saint there was almost a surfeit of material. Ignatius has transported others beside me. Paul Van Dyke, the Protestant historian, has written a most useful book about him, as has the Englishman Christopher Hollis, whose recent work, *The Jesuits,* is as entertaining as it is informative.

Anny Latour's *The Borgias* provided fodder also for my references to that family's rapacious career. Other useful works were Ronald Knox's *Enthusiasm,* a prodigious if prejudiced volume; *Autobiography* by the Mahatma

Gandhi; Mabel R. Brailsford's *A Tale of Two Brothers,* a popular history of John and Charles Wesley; E. Harris Habison's *The Christian Scholar in the Age of the Reformation; The Letters of Francis de Sales,* edited by George T. Eggleston; *The Confessions of Saint Augustine* as translated by F. J. Sheed; several biographies of both Teresa of Avila (including a translation of her own writings by E. Allison Peers) and Francis of Assisi, who has appealed to writers from his own day to this. I was also able to enjoy and to use Anne Fremantle's lively translations of obscure sources for such people as Jerome and Augustine in her *Treasury of Early Christianity;* V. Sackville-West's *The Eagle and the Dove; The Lives of the Artists* by Giorgio Vasari as translated by E. L. Seeley; and a vivacious little collection called *A Bedside Book of Saints* by Aloysius Roche.

Indeed, after having trudged through nearly three thousand pages of the *Lives,* most of my other research formed only what the English call "a good read." Florence Nightingale brought me once more to Cecil Woodham-Smith's classic book about her as well as to Lytton Strachey's irreverent essay in *Eminent Victorians.* I read Evelyn Waugh on Campion, Sheila Kaye-Smith on Rose, Chesterton on Francis of Assisi. Concerning Catherine of Siena there was an embarrassment of riches, among her more distinguished biographers being Alice Curtayne, Johannes Jorgensen, and Sigrid Undset.

Secular history, both English and European, mentions the saints again and again since they played a very large part in the civilizing of the Continent and the British Isles, and by studying that history I was able to see them in perspective as political forces, as opposed to Butler's constant focus on their religious characters. Such a figure as Bernard of Clairvaux, for instance, I found discussed in any number of books, one of the best being Amy Kelly's admirable *Eleanor of Aquitaine.* In order to understand the singularly South American quality of Rose, I had the pleasure of rereading Prescott's *Conquest of Peru.* For the

chapter about Paul, I leaned a little on Claude Tres-
montant's *Saint Paul*, but chiefly on the New Testament
and the Epistles themselves.

But dozens of other volumes gave me a line here, a
phrase there, and are too varied to list. After all, as you
must by this time have recognized, mine is not biography
but a collection of opinions, certainly fallible and perhaps,
in instances, wrong-headed.

But if I have done nothing more than dislodge some
of these strange, endearing people from their frozen pos-
tures in hagiography, I am content.

Some Saints, Their Dates, and Feast Days

Albert the Great: Albertus Magnus. Born in Swabia in 1193; died at Cologne in 1280. Feast day: November 15.

Alphonsus de Ligouri: born near Naples in 1696; died in 1787. Feast day: August 2.

Ambrose: born in Gaul in 340; died in 397. Feast day: December 7.

Anthony: born in Upper Egypt c. 251; died in 350. Feast day: January 17.

Audrey (Etheldreda): died in 679. Feast day: June 23.

Augustine: born in North Africa in 354; died in 430. Feast day: August 28.

Benedict: born in Northumbria; died in 690. Feast day: January 12.

Bernard of Clairvaux: born near Dijon in 1090; died in 1153. Feast day: August 20.

Boniface: born in Devonshire in 680; died at Dokkum in 754. Feast day: June 5.

Brendan: born in 483; died at Enach Duin in 577 or 583. Feast day: May 16.

Catherine of Siena: born at Siena in 1347; died in 1380. Feast day: April 30.

Charles Borromeo: born in 1538; died in 1584. Feast day: November 4.

Clare: born at Assisi in 1193; died in 1253. Feast day: August 12.

Columba: born at Gartan, Scotland, c. 521; died in 597. Feast day: June 9.

Dominic: born at Calaruega, Spain, c. 1170; died in 1221. Feast day: August 4.

Edmund Campion: Blessed. Born in London in 1540; died at Tyburn in 1581. Feast day: December 1.

Francis Borgia: born at Ganda in Aragon in 1510; died in 1572. Feast day: October 10.

Francis de Sales: born in Savoy in 1567; died in 1622. Feast day: January 20.

Francis of Assisi: born at Assisi in 1181 or 1182; died in 1226. Feast day: October 4.

Francis of Paola: born in Paola in Calabria in 1416; died at Plessis-les-Tours in 1507. Feast day: April 2.

Francis Xavier: born in Navarre in 1506; died on island of Sancian in 1552. Feast day: December 3.

Hilda of Whitby: died in 680. Feast day: November 17.

Ignatius of Loyola: born in castle of Loyola, Spain, in 1491; died in 1556. Feast day: July 31.

Jane Frances de Chantal: born at Dijon in 1572; died in 1641. Feast day: August 21.

Jerome: born at Stridon in Dalmatia c. 342; died in 420. Feast day: September 30.

Joan Delanoue: Blessed. Born in 1666; died in 1736. Feast day: August 17.

Joan of Arc: born at Domrémy in 1412; died at Rouen in 1431. Feast day: May 30.

John Bosco: born in 1815; died in 1888. Feast day: January 31.

John of the Cross: born in province of Old Castile in 1542; died at Ubeda in 1591. Feast day: November 24.

Laurence O'Toole: born near Castledermot, Ireland, in 1128; died at Eu in Normandy in 1180. Feast day: November 14.

Lioba: died in 780. Feast day: September 28.

Louisa de Marillac: born in 1591; died in 1660. Feast day: March 15.

Margaret of Scotland: born in exile from England c. 1046; died in 1093. Feast day: November 16.

Martin de Porres: Blessed. Born in Lima in 1579; died in 1639. Feast day: November 5.

Martin of Tours: born in Upper Pannonia; died in 397. Feast day: November 11.

Monica: born in North Africa in 332; died at Ostia in 387. Feast day: May 4.

Olaf: died at Stiklestad in 1030. Feast day: July 29.

Patrick: born c. 389; died at Saul on Strangford Lough c. 461. Feast day: March 17.

Paul: feast day: June 29.

Philip Neri: born at Florence in 1515; died in 1595. Feast day: May 26.

Pius V: born in Piedmont in 1504; died in 1572. feast day: May 5.

Pius X: born in Venetia in 1835; died in 1914. Feast day: September 3.

Radegund: died in 587. Feast day: August 13.

Robert Bellarmine: born at Montepulciano in 1542; died in 1621. Feast day: May 13.

Rose of Lima: born in Lima in 1586; died in 1617. Feast day: August 30.

Simeon Stylites: born in Cilicia c. 389; died in 495. Feast day: January 5.

Teresa: born at Avila in 1515; died in 1582. Feast day: October 15.

Theresa of Lisieux: born at Alençon in 1873; died in 1897. Feast day: October 3.

Thomas à Becket: born in London in 1118; died at Canterbury in 1170. Feast day: December 29.

Thomas Aquinas: born at Rocca Secca, near Aquino, c. 1225; died in 1274. Feast day: March 7.

Thomas More: born in London in 1478; died in 1535. Feast day: July 9.

Vincent de Paul: born in 1580; died in 1660. Feast day: July 19.

Index

Abelard, Peter, 129, 132
Acts of the Apostles, 40–41
Adamnan, 194, 197
Adeodatus, 160–64
Agnes, 104
Agostino, Fra, 183
Aiden, 197
Alaric, 164, 194
Albert the Great, *see* Albertus Magnus
Albertus Magnus, 31, 147–50
Albigensians, 129–30
Albinus, 60
Alcala, University of, 176
Aldemar, 78–79
Alexander VI, Pope, 63–67, 74
Alexander the Great, 88
Alfonso, Nicholas, 179–84, 188
Alonzo, Cardinal, *see* Callixtus III, Pope
Alphonsus de Liguori, 30, 92–93
Amadis de Gaul, 169
Ambrose, 21, 161, 203
Ancina, Juvenal, *see* Juvenal Ancina
Ancren Rule, The, 78
Angelico, Fra, 20, 31, 56

Anthony of Egypt, 30, 173–74, 197
Anthony Grassi, 123
Anthony of Padua, 16, 21
Antoninus, 56–57
Apuleius, 158
Aquinas, Thomas, *see* Thomas Aquinas
Aristotle, 88, 149, 158, 164, 178
Atahualpa, 134–36
Attila, 194
Attwater, Donald, 205
Audrey, *see* Etheldreda
Augsburg Confessions, 119
Augustine, 18, 21, 24, 31, 36, 39, 92, 121, 158–65, 167, 169, 177, 196–97, 212, 216
Augustine of Kent, 196
Austen, Jane, 111, 123

Bach, Johann Sebastian, 32, 204
Bacon, Roger, 149
Balzac, Honoré, 180
Barat, Madeleine Sophie, *see* Madeleine Sophie Barat
Baylon, Paschal, *see* Paschal Baylon

Becket, Thomas à, _see_ Thomas Becket
Bede, 21, 31, 102, 103, 197
Bedford, Francis Russell, Earl of, 156
Beethoven, Ludwig, 28
Bellarmine, Robert, _see_ Robert Bellarmine
Benedict, 27, 35, 86, 92, 195
Benedict of Amiane, 121
Benedictines, 182
Benen, 194
Benincasa, Giacomo, 107
Benincasa, Lapa, 107, 110
Benno, Brother, 81–82
Berchmans, John, _see_ John Berchmans
Bernanos, George, 37
Bernard of Clairvaux, 29, 80, 92, 127–33, 140, 143–44
Bertilla Boscardin, 31
Bobadillo, _see_ Alfonso, Nicholas
Bona, Sister, 89
Boniface, 21, 34, 93–94, 104
Book of Common Prayer, The, 152
Book of Kells, 201
Book of Martyrs, 137
Borgia, Caesar, 65–67
Borgia, Charles, 72
Borgia, Eleanor, 71
Borgia, Francis, _see_ Francis Borgia
Borgia, Juan, 65–67
Borgia, Lucretia, 65–66
Borgia, Peter, 65–66
Borgia, Rodrigo, _see_ Alexander VI, Pope
Borromeo, Charles, _see_ Charles Borromeo
Boscardin, Bertilla, _see_ Bertilla Boscardin
Bosco, John, _see_ John Bosco
Brailsford, Mabel, 221
Brendan, 92, 194, 197

Bridget, 23–24, 194
Bridget of Sweden, 99
Brodrick, James, 30–32, 67, 70, 74, 168, 178, 184, 195
Burghley, William Cecil, Lord, 153
Butler, Alban, 34, 62, 79, 94–95, 131, 138, 140, 141, 154, 203

Cabrini, Mother, _see_ Mother Cabrini
Caedmon, 104
Caesar, Julius, 174
Caesaria, 104
Caesarius of Arles, 59
Calendar and Collects, Epistles, and Gospels for the Lesser Feasts and Fasts and for Special Occasions, The, 203
Callixtus III, Pope, 64–65
Calpurnius, 192
Calvin, John, 39–40
Calvinists, 96
Campano, 65
Campion, Edmund, _see_ Edmund Campion
"Campion's Brag," 155
Camus, Jean Pierre, Bishop of Belley, 27–28
Canisius, Peter, _see_ Peter Canisius
Canmore, Malcolm, 105
Canticles, 174
Capac Huayna, _see_ Huayna Capac
Carmelites, 95, 101, 117
Carroll, Daniel, 187
Carroll, John, Bishop, 187
Carthusian Rule, 59
Caterinati, 108
Catherine the Great, 187
Catherine of Ricci, 92
Catherine of Siena, 16, 99, 107–109, 133, 145–46, 207

Cato, 159

Catullus, 174

Cecil, Sir William, *see* Burghley, Lord

Ceowulf, 58

Cervantes Saavedra, Miguel de, 166

Chantal, Jane, *see* Jane Chantal

Charlemagne, 121, 205

Charles Borromeo, 23, 118–119, 127

Charles V, Emperor, 68

Christina the Astonishing, 22–23

Christopher, 22

Chrysostom, John, *see* John Chrysostom

Church of England, 42, 219–220

Ciaran, 82–83, 194, 197

Cîteaux, 131

City of God, The, 165

Clare, 23, 88–91

Claver, Peter, *see* Peter Claver

Clement XIV, Pope, 187–88

Cleopatra, 32

Cluny, Abbey of, 37

Colman of Galway, 83, 195

Columba of Iona, 21, 76, 82–83, 194, 197–201

Columbanus, 194, 197

Columbus, Christopher, 63, 167

Columkill, *see* Columba of Iona

Commentaries of Caesar, 174

Company of Jesus, *see* Jesuits

Confessions of Augustine, 158–62, 165

Confessions of Patrick, 193

Confucianism, 185

Confucius, 186, 203

Council of Trent, 185, 188–189, 203

Counter-Reformation, 180, 189

Crashaw, Richard, 102

Crimean War, 209–11

Cromwell, Oliver, 17, 152, 191

Curé d'Ars, 31

Cuthbert, 84–85

Cyran the Abbot, 33

Dalmatius Moner, 30

Daniel, Book of, 81

Dante Alighieri, 31

Datius, 22

Dawson, Christopher, 93

Decem Rationes, 155–56

De Chardin, Teilhard, 183

De Clare, Richard Fitz-Gilbert, Earl of Pembroke, 192, 201

De Flores, Caspar, 138

De Flores, Marie, 138

De Gourmont, Remy, 90

Deicelus, 121

Delanoue, Joan, *see* Joan Delanoue

De Marillac, Louise, *see* Louise de Marillac

Demosthenes, 153

Desert Fathers, 33, 57, 121, 140, 197, 212

Dialogues of Catherine, The, 109

Diarmuid, King, 199

Divina Commedia, see "Paradiso"

Dominic, 15, 21, 57

Dominicans, 57, 123, 148, 150, 173

Domnus, Patriarch of Antioch, 142

Donne, John, 203

Douay, University of, 153

"Dove of the Church," *see* Columba of Iona

Drake, Sir Francis, 151

Drexel, Katharine, *see* Katharine Drexel

Edmund of Abingdon, 88

Edmund Campion, 151–57

Edward the Confessor, 105

Edwin, King, 60

Egbert, Archbishop of York, 19

Elburga, 104

Eleanor of Aquitane, 128

Elisha, 21

Elizabeth I, 76, 151–53, 154–157

Emerson, Ralph, 154

Enda, 194

Enthusiasm, 40

Epistles of Paul, 40–42, 43, 45–46, 47–49, 163–64, 169; Corinthians, 40, 44, 48; Galatians, 44, 47

Erasmus, Desiderius, 116, 129

Ethelbert of Kent, 59

Etheldreda, 105–6

Ethne, 194

Eudoxia, Empress, 88

Fabiola, 121–22

Fabre, Peter, *see* Peter Fabre

Felix of Nola, 82

Ferdinand of Aragon, King, 63, 66

Finbarr, 85, 194

Finnian, 194, 198–99

Firmatus, William, *see* William Firmatus

Flieder, Pastor, 209

Flowers of the Saints, 169

Fortunatus, Venantius, *see* Venantius Fortunatus

Foxe, John, 137

Francis of Assisi, 15, 18, 25, 28, 33–34, 37, 54, 56, 74, 76–79, 88–90, 96, 115, 122, 158, 174, 203

Francis Borgia, 26, 63–65, 66–74, 185

Francis de Sales, 17, 21, 24, 27–28, 30–31, 80–81, 87, 95–97, 146

Francis of Paula, 80

Francis Xavier, 18–19, 30–32, 34, 87, 127, 179–85, 188–90

Franciscans, 176, 182

Frederick the Great, 187

French Revolution, 110–12, 169, 215

Freud, Sigmund, 160

Gaiseric, 165, 194

Galilei, Galileo, 55–56, 150

Gandhi, Mahatma, 33, 211–215, 221

Gandia, University of, 70

Gandulf of Binasco, 77

Garibaldi, Giuseppe, 84

Gemman, Master, 198

Gentlemen of Stonyhurst, *see* Jesuits

Gerasimus the Abbot, 78

Gibbon, Edward, 20

Gilbert of Sempringham, 81

Gilbertines, 81

Giles, 33

Godfrey de la Haye, 59

Godfrey Zonderdonk, *see* Godfrey de la Haye

Godruc of Finchale, 76, 80

Gordon Riots, 219

Gothard, 22

Graham, Billy, 142

Grande Chartreuse, 59

Grassi, Anthony, *see* Anthony Grassi

Great Providence House, 61

Great Synod of 664, 103

Greco, El, 39

Gregory the Great, Pope, 191

Gregorian College, 73

Grigio, 83–84

Grimonia, 30
Gudric, 36
Guevara, Che, 222
Gummarus, 58–59
Gutzlaff, Charles, 186

Helenus of Egypt, 82
Henry VIII, 122, 151
Herbert, George, 203
Herbert, Sidney, 91, 207–209
Hilda of Whitby, 20, 99, 102–104, 106
Hildegard, 104
Hitler, Adolph, 147
Hollis, Christopher, 175
Homer, 160
Hopkins, Gerard Manley, 183
Howard, Philip, Earl of Arundel, 157
Huascar, 135, 136
Huayna Capac, 134
Hugh, Abbot of Grenoble, 56
Hugh the Great, 37
Hugh of Lincoln, 34, 59, 61, 81
Humbaline, 132

Ignatius of Loyola, 26, 35, 70–74, 82, 87, 115, 118–119, 166–85, 187–90, 214, 216
Innocent III, Pope, 205
Innocent VIII, Pope, 66
Inquisition, 26, 73, 100, 118, 150, 177–79
Interior Castle, The, 101–102, 174
Isabella I, 63, 167
Ita, 194
Ivo of Kermartin, 57

James, William, 28, 172
James of Cerqueto, 81
Jane Chantal, 87, 95–97
Jansen, Cornelius, 42

Javouhey, Balthazar, 110–11
Javouhey, Mother Anne Marie, 99, 110–14, 143, 207
Jerome, 20–21, 23, 30, 36, 87–88, 94, 121–22, 164, 177, 196, 203
Jesuits, 18, 26, 70–74, 82, 152, 154–58, 166, 173, 180–81, 182, 184–90
Joan of Arc, 24, 25, 64, 93, 99
Joan Delanoue, 60–61, 62
Joan of Orvieto, 35
Jogues, 34
John Berchmans, 116
John Bosco, 24, 83–84, 120–121, 143
John of the Cross, 21, 26, 84, 95, 117, 174
John of God, 18
John Chrysostom, 88
John Massias of Lima, 82
John of Saxony, 118
John XXIII, Pope, 64, 143, 206
John of Vercelli, 123
Johnson, Samuel, 32, 183
Joseph of Anchieta, 80
Judaism, 41, 43
Jude, 16
Julian, Emperor, 30
Juvenal Ancina, 59–60

Katherine Drexel, 53–54
Keats, John, 28
Kennedy, President John Fitzgerald, 222
Kevin, 194, 197
King, Martin Luther, 205, 222
Knox, Ronald, 40

Ladies of Charity, 91
Laurence O'Toole, 33, 201
Law, William, 20, 217
Laynez, Diego, 73–74, 179, 181–84, 188

Leicester, Robert Dudley, Earl of, 153, 156–57
Leo I, Pope, 142
Lioba, 16, 93–94, 99, 104, 121, 127
Lippo, Brandolini, 65–66
Lives of the Saints, 34, 79, 119
Louis VII, 128
Louis IX, 19
Louis-Philippe, 99
Louise de Marillac, 91–92
Ludovic Pavone, 119
Luke, 41
Lull, Raymond, *see* Raymond Lull
Luther, Martin, 66, 119–20, 148, 175, 179, 185, 221

Madeleine Sophie Barat, 123
Malo, 76
Manichaeism, 161, 164
Manichees, 19, 161
Manning, Cardinal, 207
Marcian, Emperor, 142
Margaret of Cortona, 35
Margaret of Scotland, 105–106
Marie, Mother, *see* Mother Marie
Marie Celeste, 92–93
Mariolino, 35
Martin de Porres, 79, 92, 137
Martin of Tours, 29, 33, 53
Mary, Blessed Virgin, 171
Mary of Egypt, 18
Mary of the Gael, *see* Bridget
Mary Magdalene, 18
Mary Mazzarello, 116
Maryknoll Missioners, 34
Massias, John of Lima, *see* John Massias of Lima
Mather, Cotton, 150
Maugham, Somerset, 175
Mazzarello, Mary, *see* Mary Mazzarello

Mechtildis, 36
Melanchthon, Philipp, 119–20
Melania, 92
Merton, Thomas, 129
Methodism, 42, 216
Methodists, 218
Michelangelo, 20, 28
Mildred, 104
Mirror of Perfection, 78
Mithras, 43
Moner, Dalmatius, *see* Dalmatius Moner
Monica, 159, 162–64
Montagu, Ashley, 45
Montaigu, College of, 178
Montserrat, 171–80
More, Jane, 60
More, Thomas, *see* Thomas More
Moses the Black, 36
Mother Anne Marie Javouhey, *see* Javouhey, Mother Anne Marie
Mother Cabrini, 127
Mother Marie, 16

Nelson, Horatio, Lord, 151
Neri, Philip, *see* Philip Neri
Neri de Landoccio, 108
Nero, Emperor, 48
Newton, Isaac, 149
Nicholas, 22
Nicholas V, Pope, 64
Nicholas Owen, 152
Nicholas the Pilgrim, 22, 59
Niebuhr, Reinhold, 180, 189
Nightingale, Florence, 91, 111, 207–211, 215, 221
Nightingale, Parthe, 208–209
Nonnatus, Raymond, *see* Raymond Nonnatus

Ochoa, Father, 82
O'Connor, Rory, King, 201
Odoacer, 194

Oglethorpe, James Edward, 216–18, 221

Olaf, 146–47, 205

Olympias, 88

Origen, 121

O'Toole, Laurence, *see* Laurence O'Toole

Ovid, 174

Owen, Nicholas, *see* Nicholas Owen

Oxford, University of, 152–53, 217

Ozanam, Frédéric, 87

Paine, Thomas, 169

Palladius, 192–93

Palloti, Vincent, *see* Vincent Palloti

"*Paradiso*," 31

Paris, University of, 149, 178

Parsons, Robert, 154–56

Pascal, Blaise, 26, 187, 205

Paschal Baylon, 116

Patricius, 159

Patrick, 80, 165, 192–93, 196

Paul, 34, 40–49, 109, 117, 163, 174, 189, 204

Paul III, Pope, 183–84

Paula, 23, 30, 87–88, 94

Pavone, Ludovic, *see* Ludovic Pavone

Pelagia, 62–63

Pelagius, 164, 196

Pepin, 58

Peter, 34, 37, 41, 44

Peter Canisius, 188

Peter Claver, 34

Peter Fabre, 179–84, 189

Petroc, 84

Philip Neri, 20, 24, 80–81, 84, 92, 119–20

Philip II, 68, 101

Pinchon, William, *see* William Pinchon

Pius V, Pope, 76, 119, 151–52

Pius X, Pope, 24, 57–58, 122

Pius XI, Pope, 150

Pizarro, Francisco, 134–36

Plato, 163

Pliny, 149

Poor Clares, 89–90, 115

Portiuncula, 89–90

Prescott, William H., 136

Punic Wars, 159

Radegund, Abbess of Poitiers, 94–95, 104

Raleigh, Sir Walter, 151

Raymond Lull, 36

Raymond Nonnatus, 34

Reformation, 26, 119–20, 134, 137, 151, 175, 177, 184, 203

Reign of Terror, 110

Ricci, Matteo, 185–86

Richard of Wyche, 55, 80

Richard the Lion-Hearted, 81

Robert Bellarmine, 24, 55

Rock, 84

Rodriguez, Simon, 179–84, 186

Roman Catholic Priests of Maryland, *see* Jesuits

Rose of Lima, 23, 29, 79, 92, 133–34, 137–40, 143–44, 145, 207

Rufiana, 23

Rufinus, 121

Sabrinus, 22

Saint Gall, monastery of, 31

Saint Joseph of Cluny, *see* Sisters of Saint Joseph

Sainte Barbe, College of, 178

Saladin, 75–76

Salamanca, University of, 177

Salesians, 83–84, 120

Salmerson, Alfonso, 179–84

Saul, *see* Paul

Savonarola, Girolamo, 66

Scholastica, 27, 86, 92

Schweitzer, Albert, 205
Sechnall, 194
*Serious Call to a Devout and
   Holy Life, A,* 8, 217
Servetus, 39
Shakespeare, William, 28, 39
Simeon Stylites, 139–44, 145
Sisters of Charity, 91
Sisters of Saint Joseph, 111
Society of Jesus, *see* Jesuits
Society of the Sacred Heart,
   123
Solomon, 96
Southwell, Robert, 183
Spiridion, 35
"Spiritual Exercises" of Igna-
   tius Loyola, 70, 117, 174–
   175, 176, 181–82, 185
Spock, Benjamin, 138
Stephen, 131
Stephen (martyr), 41
Strachey, Lytton, 207
Strongbow, *see* de Clare,
   Richard Fitz-Gilbert, Earl
   of Pembroke
Stylites, Simeon, *see* Simeon
   Stylites
Swift, Jonathan, 121
Synod of Whitby, 195

Tagaste, 161–62
Taylor, F. Sherwood, 148
Tempier, Stephen, Bishop of
   Paris, 149
Tennyson, Alfred, Lord, 16
Terence, 158
Teresa of Avila, 19, 21, 24,
   26, 29–30, 74, 94–95, 99–
   102, 109, 117–18, 123, 158,
   174, 206, 216
Theodosius, Emperor, 142
Theon of Thebaud, 85
Theophilus, 88
Theresa of Lisieux, 23, 27, 31
Thirty-Nine Articles, 153

Thomas, 24, 34, 41
Thomas Aquinas, 18–19, 24,
   26, 31, 39, 69, 148–50, 158,
   164, 175, 216
Thomas Becket, 25, 76
Thomas More, 20–21, 25, 31,
   60, 116, 122, 151
Thoreau, Henry David, 29
Toxotius, 23
*Treatise of Divine Providence,
   A,* 109
Trevelyan, George Macaulay,
   191, 197, 201
Trinity College, Dublin, 201
Tutilo, 31

Ubald of Florence, 62
Uncle Tom's Cabin, 169
Urban V, Pope, 145

Valentine, 21
Vanni, Andrew, 108
*Varieties of Religious Experi-
   ence,* 28
Vasari, Giorgio, 21
Venantius Fortunatus, 94–95
Victoria, Queen, 207, 210
Vincent de Paul, 36, 54–55,
   61, 90–91, 143
Vincent Palloti, 33
Virgil, 160
Visitandines, 92
Vitus, 121

Walaricus, 78
Walburga, 105
Walpole, Henry, 157
Walpurgis, *see* Walburga
Way of Perfection, The, 101
Wenceslaus, 121
Wesley, Charles, 216–20
Wesley, John, 20, 32, 42, 175,
   215–21
Wesley, Samuel, 217
Wesley, Susanna, 217

West, Rebecca, 159

Wilberforce, William, 203, 216

Wilde, Oscar, 116

William Firmatus, 79–80

William Pinchon, 33

William the Conqueror, 78

Woolf, Virginia, 98–99

Wulfstan, 203–204

Xavier, Francis, *see* Francis Xavier

OTHER IMAGE BOOKS

OUR LADY OF FATIMA – William Thomas Walsh (D1) – $1.25

DAMIEN THE LEPER – John Farrow (D3) – $1.25

MR. BLUE – Myles Connolly. Modern classic about a contemporary St. Francis (D5) – 75¢

CHRIST THE LORD – Gerard S. Sloyan (E6) – 95¢

PEACE OF SOUL – Fulton J. Sheen (D8) – $1.25

THE PERFECT JOY OF ST. FRANCIS – Felix Timmermans (D11) – $1.95

THE IMITATION OF CHRIST – Thomas à Kempis. Edited with an Introduction by Harold C. Gardiner, S.J. (D17) – $1.45

ST. FRANCIS OF ASSISI – Johannes Jorgensen (D22) – $1.45

THE SIGN OF JONAS – Thomas Merton (D31) – $1.95

LIGHT ON THE MOUNTAIN: The Story of La Salette – John S. Kennedy (D33) – 95¢

SAINT THOMAS AQUINAS – G. K. Chesterton (D36) – $1.45

THE ART OF BEING HUMAN – William McNamara, O.C.D. (E45) – $1.25

THE STORY OF THE TRAPP FAMILY SINGERS – Maria Augusta Trapp (D46) – 95¢

ST. FRANCIS OF ASSISI – G. K. Chesterton (D50) – $1.25

VIPER'S TANGLE – François Mauriac. A novel of evil and redemption (D51) – 95¢

THE LEFT HAND OF GOD – William E. Barrett (E55) – 95¢

THE AUTOBIOGRAPHY OF ST. THÉRÈSE OF LISIEUX: The Story of a Soul – Translated by John Beevers. An Image Original (D56) – $1.25

THE CITY OF GOD – St. Augustine. Edited by Vernon J. Bourke. Introduction by Étienne Gilson. Specially abridged (D59) – $2.45

ASCENT OF MT. CARMEL – St. John of the Cross. Trans. and ed. by E. Allison Peers (D63) – $1.95

RELIGION AND THE RISE OF WESTERN CULTURE – Christopher Dawson (D64) – $1.95

THE LITTLE FLOWERS OF ST. FRANCIS – Translated by Raphael Brown (D69) – $1.75

DARK NIGHT OF THE SOUL – St. John of the Cross. Edited and translated by E. Allison Peers (D78) – $1.25

ORTHODOXY – G. K. Chesterton (D84) – $1.25

THE LIFE OF TERESA OF JESUS: The Autobiography of St. Teresa of Avila. Trans. and ed. by E. Allison Peers (D96) – $1.95

THE CONFESSIONS OF ST. AUGUSTINE – Translated with an Introduction by John K. Ryan (D101) – $1.75

These prices subject to change without notice

▲ 74–1